CONTENTS

SUCCE

CTION YEAR

SUCCEEDING IN THE INDUCTION YEAR

Second edition

Neil Simco

First published in 2000 by Learning Matters Ltd.
Reprinted in 2002.
Second edition published in 2003.

British Library Cataloguing in Publication Data
A CIP record for this book is available from the British Library.

ISBN 1 903300 93 2

Cover design by Code 5 Design Associates Ltd
Project management by Deer Park Productions
Typeset and illustrated by PDQ Typesetting
Printed and bound in Great Britain by Bell & Bain Ltd, Glasgow

Learning Matters Ltd
33 Southernhay East
Exeter EXI INX
Tel: 01392 215560
Email: info@learningmatters.co.uk
www.learningmatters.co.uk

This book has been written with one central aim, namely to provide you with clear, supportive information which will enable you to derive as much professional benefit from the induction period as possible. It is not a book about 'surviving the induction year' because this has negative connotations. It *is* a book about managing and antici-pating the year so that you make the most of this critically important period in your professional life. It is also a book which aims to ensure that the demands of the induc-tion period are fully acknowledged. It shows how you can develop your skills, competences and understandings within the context of your day-to-day teaching, not as a 'bolt-on extra'. *Succeeding in the Induction Year* aims to be principled and inno-vative, but also located in a reality which newly qualified teachers will recognise.

The material will be of interest to a number of different audiences. Firstly and obviously it will be of interest if you are a newly qualified teacher – primary or secondary – either at the start of the year or part-way through. The book has been designed so that you can read it from cover to cover to gain a perception of the year as a whole, or alternatively you may wish to dip into different sections at various times in the year. Secondly, the book will be relevant if you are a trainee teacher (whatever course you are following). I aim to show the relationship between initial teacher training and induction, and a particular focus for this is the Career Entry and Development Profile (CEDP). Beyond this I think the book will be of interest to those involved in managing the induction year – induction tutors, LEA advisers, headteachers and ITT tutors – because if they are to be effective in their work, they need to see the induc-tion period from the perspective of NQTs.

You will see that the book centres very much on the detail of the statutory arrangements for the induction period. It explores the implications of these for newly qualified teachers and it anticipates issues and identifies opportunities. I have chosen to do this because I believe the national framework will have a very significant impact on induction practice and that while there will always be the issue of consis-tency between one school and the next, NQTs' experience of the induction period in 2004 is likely to be very different from my experience as a probationary teacher. *Succeeding in the Induction Year* is about interpreting the national framework for induc-tion so that it has maximum impact on the experience of that year for individual NQTs. In this sense the book aims to be positive and forward-looking.

I think that there are three major strands which run through the book. The first of these stresses the responsibility of newly qualified teachers to be active in framing the induction period. The induction year should not be 'done to' NQTs but with them.

NQTs are professionals and have an entitlement to contribute fully to their own professional development. They should have the power to define direction and activity for professional growth, but they also need to acknowledge their responsibility to be proactive when support is less than satisfactory or in being rigorous in their self-assessment. However, it is also true that a balance should be struck, as success in the induction period shouldn't depend on the NQT constantly reminding, agenda setting and ensuring compliance with the various elements of the national framework. The school has defined responsibilities and these need to be fully acknowledged. Most schools will have in place systems for NQTs, including programmes of professional support, arrangements for assessment meetings and a wide range of opportunities for professional development. The extent to which the induction year is positive and fruitful ultimately depends on all parties, but particularly NQTs and mentors for NQTs (called induction tutors), taking their share of responsibility.

A second strand which is emphasised throughout the book is the idea of *individual* professional development. This is a central aspect of the national arrangements for induction and was embedded within the thinking of the TTA and DfEE from the early development phases of the current national system. I think that this is a good principle. It acknowledges that no two teachers will have exactly the same professional needs and it creates an expectation of individually tailored induction programmes based on a thorough analysis of individuals' strengths and priorities for further development. Additionally it suggests that while themed courses for newly qualified teachers (focused, for example, on behaviour management or Special Needs) have their place, they are not in themselves sufficient. The structured, individual conversations between newly qualified teachers and induction tutors are of critical importance. Throughout the book I have placed strong emphasis on the individual, both during the latter stages of initial teacher training and in regard to the kinds of professional support which should form the bedrock of the induction period itself.

The final strand which is emphasised is the linkage between initial teacher training and induction. My experience of the old probationary year did not involve any such linkage in any explicit way. It was almost as if ITT and my first post were two separate worlds. This was an opportunity missed. At the end of ITT I had a clear idea of which aspects of teaching I was reasonably good at, which less so. I wanted the opportunity to make this explicit but instead probation felt like starting again! For me it wasn't until my second year of teaching that I was able to understand how I was translating values and beliefs about teaching and learning into my actual classroom practice. In the national induction arrangements the Career Entry and Development Profile (CEDP) has the potential to make individual, specific links between ITT and induction. Whether this potential is realised depends on the first strand outlined above, and in particular whether the NQT is able to take a share of the responsibility for their own professional development, stimulated by the induction tutor's mentoring.

You will see that the book is divided into five chapters. Apart from this introduction it is written 'to' NQTs because I wish to stimulate a dialogue with them and I thought a personal approach would be most appropriate. The first chapter provides an overview of the current induction arrangements and the development of the system. It is different in nature from other chapters in the book as it is concerned with background and context and in this sense it does not focus on the practical day-to-day considerations. I have included it because for many new teachers the induction year will be a highly significant part of their professional biography. To experience this year without understanding something of its context seems inappropriate and incomplete. I also believe that part of being 'professional' involves more than managing the day to day: it is concerned with an understanding of the circumstances in which we work.

Chapter 2 focuses on the latter part of initial teacher training. Its main focus is the CEDP, particularly those parts which are to be completed prior to qualification. It aims to ensure that readers see that the CEDP is potentially an extremely useful document in the induction period and that to give it thorough attention during the latter part of ITT is an important, perhaps critical part of preparation. The chapter also anticipates the induction year, particularly in regard to elements of the new arrangements and how prospective NQTs can anticipate these and make an appropriate response.

The next two chapters, 3 and 4, are the core chapters of the book. I was involved in preparing the national support materials for induction (TTA 1999a) and these chapters build on some of this work and take it further. Chapter 3 is focused on monitoring and support. It establishes the nature of support and focuses particularly on the role of observation. It considers the components of a professional development programme, discusses the use which should be made of the CEDP in the induction year and identifies effective practice in professional review meetings. The chapter is very practical in orientation and will be of benefit to NQTs who wish to be clear and focused about the nature of their entitlement. Chapter 4 focuses on the assessment of the induction period. This is, of course, an area that is (understandably) one of concern to many NQTs and the chapter aims to 'demystify' this process so that NQTs can see exactly what it involves. It makes the very clear assertion that what it doesn't involve is a rerun of a final block placement!

The final chapter of the book is concerned with NQTs' stories, real accounts of the induction period from a range of perspectives. I have chosen to include these stories as I wished to ensure a sense of realism, an honest, straightforward account of the 'highs' and 'lows'.

Acknowledgements

Throughout the book, but particularly in Chapters 2, 3 and 4, you will see that I have included a large number of examples, proformas and case histories. My aim here is to ensure that you have a sense of the book being about the induction year as 'real life'. In many respects these examples are the heart and soul of the book and I wish to acknowledge contributions while also mentioning that in all the examples pseudonyms have been used. Firstly, I wish to acknowledge all the NQTs and experienced teachers whose work contributes to the book, namely those from Quarry View Primary School, Sunderland, Anchorsholme Primary School, Blackpool, Heron Hill Primary School,

Kendal and Bitterne Park School, Southampton. Your contributions have been seminal. Thanks are also due to the small team with whom I worked on the development of the national support materials for induction published by the TTA in 1999 and which formed the foundation for Chapters 3 and 4. I found this work to be creative, innovative and challenging and my understandings of induction were greatly enhanced during our discussions. Particular mention must be made of Jill Staley and John Carr at the TTA in this respect, and of Maureen Lee who was involved in the national project and who made valuable and detailed comments on an earlier draft of the book. Chris Sixsmith at St Martin's College has been a constant source of inspiration to me and my concept of induction is in no small part a result of the many discussions we have had over many years. I have valued working with Clive Carroll, also at St Martin's, who has also developed my knowledge of induction. I wish to acknowledge the DfES, the TTA and St Martin's College who have given permission for the national and institutional proformas to be reproduced in the book. Susan Cockburn, Jane Cambridge and Thora Cartwright have provided wonderful secretarial support and my wife Sam and our baby daughter Beth have allowed me the luxury of time and space to prepare the book. I am deeply grateful for that.

Neil Simco

Chapter 1:
The Induction Year: Background, Context, Opportunities and Pitfalls

In this chapter you will find:

- **outline information about the national induction arrangements;**
- **background information about the historical development of the national system for induction;**
- **an overview of the strengths and weaknesses of policy and practice in induction.**

The chapter is unlike other chapters in the book as it is concerned mostly with background and context rather than day-to-day matters.

The main purpose of this first chapter is to provide you with background information about the induction year which you may be about to start, or are part-way through. It sets the scene for the practical day-to-day support material which follows and it is concerned with the 'macro' policy level and its likely impact on your experience as a beginning teacher. The chapter considers the historical development of the induction period and argues that issues such as creating seamlessness between initial teacher training and induction have in the past few decades been difficult to address in the reality of school life. By the end of the chapter you should be able to judge whether the current induction arrangements have the potential to address some of the issues which have been problematic in earlier induction policy and practice. Will your experience be substantially different from the new teachers who have gone before? You may notice that the style of this chapter is rather different from that adopted for the remainder of the book. This is quite deliberate. I wanted to provide you with some contextual material before the practical issues which you will face are considered. In this way you will see that this chapter has something of an analytical style, while remaining chapters are written rather more directly and practically. I hope that you will find that both styles are appropriate!

Two primary teachers give their views about the nature of their experience as beginning teachers (see induction stories on page 6). Whilst it's clearly not possible to generalise from these stories, they provide an illustration of how new teachers were inducted into the profession at particular moments in particular schools. The first description relates to a period when the old probationary year was in operation; the second is concerned with a teacher who experienced the induction year when it was newly established in the early 1990s. The main difference between the probationary year and the induction year prior to 1999 was that the former was formally assessed and a pass was necessary to gain access to the profession while the latter was not.

1986 induction story

Peter undertook his probationary year in a large primary school in the mid-1980s. He recalls that he was welcomed into the school and had plenty of informal support from a colleague who worked in the upper junior department. There were additional opportunities to attend two valuable LEA courses for probationary teachers. Foremost in his memory are the two observations of his teaching by the headteacher and the assessment visit of the LEA probationers' co-ordinator. He also recalls that there were no criteria for this assessment, that there were few opportunities for systematic professional development – 'tutorials' – and that feedback was 'done to' rather than 'agreed with'. For him the probationary year was largely informal and low key, and marked by some background anxiety at the time of the observations.

1993 induction story

Charlotte was employed in an urban junior school for her first year of teaching in the early 1990s. She received no formal mentoring or support during her induction year, although she worked well with the parallel teacher in her unit. During the whole year she was not observed teaching (apart from during an HMI inspection), but on three occasions she was provided with an opportunity to observe other teachers in the school, although there was no agreed focus for this work. She attended four half-day courses for new teachers set up through the LEA. She describes these as 'over generalised' and 'poorly delivered'. There was no assessment of her induction year. For Charlotte the induction year was a period of rapid professional development but there was a real lack of opportunity to engage in professional dialogue. Professional development was self-generated; for example, at one point Charlotte made a list of learning strategies and over a period of time she matched her planning against them to check that there was a balance of different kinds of learning. At no point was there an opportunity to share this with other teachers.

For both Charlotte and Peter their experience of the first year of teaching was then characterised by:

- a lack of structured support and monitoring;
- a lack of opportunity for systematic, focused, individual professional development;
- a lack of explicit linkage to experiences in ITT.

Additionally, there were inconsistencies between them in terms of:

- the nature of informal support in the schools;
- the process of assessment of the year – although the contexts of probation and induction are different;
- the perceived quality of the LEA courses;
- the willingness to engage in focused self-assessment.

The two cases hence illustrate a number of the issues which the new arrangements are trying to address. What remains to be seen is whether the current developments will succeed in achieving this.

The induction arrangements in outline

1999 will be seen in the history of education as an important year in regard to the development of policy in induction. The publication of Circular 5/99, *The Induction Period for Newly Qualified Teachers* (DfEE 1999), marked a clear shift of direction in policy at national level. The Circular established two main principles and these principles are retained in the current policy framework for induction. They are:

- **national guidelines for the minimum entitlement of newly qualified teachers (NQTs) in terms of professional development and support;**
- **the summative assessment of NQTs against defined national standards.**

The remaining requirements of the induction period are identified in the Guidance and these are summarised in the box on page 8. What remains to be seen is whether you as an NQT can see these two principles relating to minimum entitlement and summative assessment reflected in your experience of the induction year. If this is the case then this will be no mean achievement. The last fifty years and more have been associated with two clear realities in induction policy and practice. The first is that there have been a number of national initiatives to develop practice in induction (McNair 1944, DES 1972, Bolam *et al.* 1975). The second is that there is a large body of research evidence which has suggested that good practice in induction has, at best, been ad hoc.

Induction policy and practice 1925–2004

I want now to move on to consider, briefly, some aspects of the history of induction policy and practice in the twentieth century. This will provide you, I hope, with some interesting background to your experience as an NQT. A summary of the main events can be seen in the box on page 9.

Tickle (1994) provides some evidence related to induction policy and practice in the first part of the twentieth century. In 1925, for example, there were attempts at national level, through the then Board of Education, to link initial training and induction, but according to Evans (1978) these attempts were abandoned due to funding difficulties. Then in 1944, the McNair Report established the principle of assessing newly qualified teachers' competence and sought to encourage the provision of professional support and monitoring in schools for these teachers. The emphasis, however, was on probation and not induction and the assessment of the NQTs was dominant over support and monitoring. While there appears to be a paucity of research evidence in the late 1940s and 1950s about the experiences of NQTs, Tickle (1994) points to a number of studies in the 1960s and early 1970s which painted a dismal picture of the characteristics of the first year of teaching (Collins 1969, Taylor and Dale 1971). It appeared that many new teachers had inadequate information, were isolated and

A Summary of the Induction Period Requirements *The Induction Period for Newly Qualified Teachers*

- The new arrangements apply to England.

- National Standards are established for the successful completion of the induction period, which build on the standards for the award of QTS.

- The induction period is the equivalent of one year's full-time teaching.

- Broadly all schools can provide an induction period, except:

  – pupil referral units

  – some schools in special measures

  – independent schools which do not teach the National Curriculum

  – further education colleges

  – private or voluntary nursery settings.

- Roles and responsibilities are established for headteachers, LEAs, induction tutors (i.e. mentors of NQTs), NQTs and the governing body.

- NQTs cannot complete the induction period by aggregating periods of short-term supply of less than a term's duration.

- NQTs have an entitlement to an induction programme which:

  – provides individual support and monitoring in relation to agreed targets in the Career Entry and Development Profile (CEDP)

  – actively involves the NQT in the planning of the programme

  – includes, for example, support from the induction tutor, observation of NQTs teaching, ongoing professional review of progress and observation of experienced teachers.

- NQTs should have 90% teaching load compared with other colleagues.

- The consistent meeting of the QTS standards and the induction standards is formally assessed at three assessment meetings in the year.

- On the rare occasions where the standards are not met this will lead to the NQT not being allowed to continue in employment in a maintained or non-maintained special school. There is an appeal procedure for these occasions.

DfES (2003)

saw the first year of teaching as concerned only with assessment of their competence rather than any systematic professional development.

It was this kind of sentiment which was endorsed in the 1972 James Report which like the McNair recommendations sought to provide proper support and monitoring of new teachers' work along with the assessment of their competence. A major difference was that there was a more equal balance between assessment and professional development. The James Report suggested that 'Nothing has impressed, or depressed, us more than the gross inadequacy of the present arrangements for the probationary year. This inadequacy has hampered even the most enlightened of current procedures

Some key events in the history of induction policy.

- 1925 Board of Education attempts to link initial training and induction.

- 1944 McNair Report establishes principle of assessing new teachers' work within a context of proper support.

- 1972 James Report seeks to establish appropriate balance between assessment and professional development in the probationary year.

- 1982, 1987, 1993 Major HMI reports question the consistency of effective provision for new teachers.

- 1992 Probation abolished by the then Secretary of State, Kenneth Clarke. Professional development is fostered.

- 1999 DfEE introduces the new induction arrangements and the idea of formally combining rigorous assessment and individual professional development.

and has sometimes left unchecked practices which are so much less enlightened as to imply incompetence and irresponsibility' (DES 1972, para 3.10). The interesting issue is that the James Report recommendations were very similar to those made by the Board of Education and the McNair Report. The issues surrounding induction policy and practice were stubbornly persistent over a very long period of time.

Between 1925 and 1972, there had effectively been three major attempts to move policy forward so that the first year of teaching had characteristics of both assessment and systematic professional development. There is evidence to suggest that the classroom reality did not always reflect this policy framework. This point is endorsed by Bolam *et al.* (1995) who refer to the period prior to and post the James Report and suggest that 'For more than a generation, there has been broad agreement, in England and Wales, between the profession, local authority employers and successive governments, that the induction of newly qualified teachers (NQTs) is still inadequate and ought to be improved' (Bolam *et al.* 1995, p. 247).

Bolam *et al.* hence imply that the position post-James was very similar to that pre-James and this is borne out by research evidence and findings from HMI inspections. The following quotations are taken from the three HMI reports on induction spanning the 1980s and early 1990s. Taken together they again raise serious issues about the quality of induction in schools, although at the margin, the reports did indicate some areas of progress in induction as the 1980s progressed.

> The majority of schools provided at least adequate and generally appropriate support, though there were many cases where they gave too little, or (less commonly) too much help. But the circumstances of the new teachers' first year were largely a matter of chance. If it is the case that the induction year is an integral part of the teacher's training, and a key element in their professional development, it is clearly unsatisfactory that its effectiveness should be so haphazard.
> (DES 1982, para 6.7)

An appreciation of the limitations of what initial training can accomplish and what induction should entail is essential. The expectations of many schools were too high and the jobs given to probationers, in secondary schools especially, were often too demanding. A substantial proportion of all schools were making no or inadequate, provision for the needs of their new teachers.

(DES 1987, para 1.41)

In practice... induction was generally informal and incidental, and frequently involved several members of staff. It also varied considerably from school to school. Three-quarters of heads reported that an induction programme had been planned, but most of the new teachers judged this provision to have been slight... Priority in induction was rarely given to pedagogical or curriculum needs. Most schools saw their role as one of support rather than of training.

(OFSTED 1993, para 5.3 and p. 38)

Available research evidence also suggested that there were ongoing difficulties with the quality and consistency of induction provision during the 1980s and early 1990s. Interestingly the same kind of issues appeared to be being raised after the abolition of the probationary year and the inception of the induction year in 1992 (DES 1992). Carré (1993), for example, found that there was a tremendous variation in NQTs' experiences of induction and that while NQTs were warmly welcomed into their schools, few inductees had opportunities for structured and individual professional development. Turner's (1982) research with experienced teachers pointed to their belief that there was little support for professional development in the then probationary year. In 1992, the then Secretary of State Kenneth Clarke announced the abolition of the probationary year to create a climate where professional development in the induction year could be fostered. In this way there was no longer to be formal assessment of the first year of teaching the results of which related to whether the new teacher would be admitted to the profession. Turner's (1994) research on the management of induction again suggests wide variation between different local education authorities (LEAs) and different schools. He does, however, suggest that the abolition of probation in 1992 had led to LEAs developing policies which moved from a laissez-faire approach to one where there was either more central control or a sharper focus on individual paths of professional development. In this sense there is much evidence of good emerging practice. Many LEAs developed portfolios to aid NQTs' professional development and encouraged systematic observation using lists of teaching competences. Additionally LEAs worked with higher education institutions to establish accreditation for NQTs and their mentors. Simco (1995) implies, however, that the issue of recognising individual needs while emerging may not have become apparent across the country at this stage in practice. At that time I wrote that 'NQTs are warmly welcomed into their schools, and... they have an acute sense of their own professional strengths and areas for development' but that 'the induction programmes and procedures do not always provide for a process of rigorous and systematic professional development' (p. 271).

In England in the 1980s and early 1990s the broad picture in induction was similar to a previous era, i.e. one where the rhetoric of policy did not reflect a consistent reality of good quality focused professional development in the induction year. This broad picture is also evident at an international level. Bleach (1998) analyses the status quo in induction in the Republic of Ireland and argues that documents from the Irish Department of Education suggested arrangements for induction were 'ad hoc and incomplete' (p. 55). Likewise Bolam (1994) argues that inductees in the USA have often received few opportunities for professional development, despite policy initiatives in the area of induction.

There is, then, an emerging picture of induction being a particularly difficult area in which to make policy changes which impact at classroom level. Lee (1993) commenting on the twenty years between the publication of the James Report in 1972 and his editorial for a special edition of the *British Journal of In-Service Education* writes that 'I could only think of two things that had been consistent over the intervening years. One was the excellence of Liverpool's football; the second was that while everybody agreed something had to be done about induction into the teaching profession, no one actually did anything' (p. 3). Bolam *et al.* (1995) comment on the national status quo in the mid-1990s arguing that there has been broad agreement amongst all stakeholders, including the profession and successive governments, that induction provision was inadequate; that there were several national attempts to improve induction, including the Teacher Induction Pilot Schemes and GEST funding for induction; and that there has been a common view about the elements of effective induction, e.g. non-contact time, structured support, observing others and being observed. There is, in short, little doubt that the practice of induction has been problematic and has been so for a very long time.

In what ways has induction been problematic?

There is also some consensus in terms of the *ways* in which induction has been problematic and perhaps this can be illustrated with reference to three key areas:

- **linkage of ITT and induction;**
- **the non-existence of individual professional support;**
- **inconsistency of provision between schools.**

The first issue is the extent to which the experience and understanding gained in initial teacher training link to the first year of teaching. Key questions here would include: are NQTs aware of their individual strengths and weaknesses at the start of this induction period, and are these carried forward in any systematic way? This is not a new issue! Evans (1978) reports that the 1925 report to the Board of Education envisaged 'the complete preliminary training as consisting of the college year and the probationary year together' (p. 4). In 1997, 72 years later, the Sutherland Report again called for the creation of structured induction arrangements which integrate the first year of teaching with ITT. In between the HMI reports of the 1980s called for closer liaison between training institutions and schools such that detailed information was available about individual NQTs' strengths and weaknesses at the point of leaving ITT.

A second way in which induction has been problematic relates to the non-existence, in many circumstances, of individual and systematic professional support. This has been an increasing issue and again can be grounded in the three HMI reports. It seems that there is some consensus that while NQTs are welcomed into their first posts, professional development is often seen in terms of informal support and reaction to events, rather than systematic school-based training. This needs to be responsive to NQTs' individual strengths and weaknesses. It needs to be proactive in response to targets which have been set with NQTs. Thompson (1991) tends to agree with this supposition and sees that it is the NQTs' lack of power and status that have meant the lack of opportunities for this systematic professional development. Additionally, on occasion, there can be a tension between NQTs' individual priorities and the priorities reflected in a school or department development plan.

In considering how induction has been problematic, there is a third area. While there needs to be a clear acknowledgement that there has been much very good practice in supporting NQTs, the issue of inconsistency of provision is also a reality. There is a great deal of evidence to suggest that there has been a strong element of luck in determining the kind of input that is experienced by NQTs. Capel (1998) reports that while the majority of NQTs in her study received adequate or better support, 'a few NQTs indicated that they had very little, or no support, that they did not feel able to ask for help or that they felt under pressure to cope without extra help' (p. 407). The findings of this small-scale study are also apparent in larger studies, including the three HMI reports and the Taylor and Dale 1971 study. From the management aspect, studies such as Bines and Boydell (1995) and Turner (1994) have shown the widespread variation in approaches which schools have taken to the management of the induction year.

There is then some consensus about the ways in which induction policy and practice has been so problematic. There are, of course, also a variety of reasons to explain why induction policy and practice has been so problematic and while a detailed consideration of these is beyond the scope of the current chapter, it is interesting to note the broad nature of these reasons. In this respect Tickle (1994) provides a useful analysis. He suggests five reasons:

- **Inadequate funding of policy initiatives.**
- **The notion that initial teacher training is increasingly concerned with the acquisition of technical skill, rather than intellectual curiosity about professional development.**
- **A national system of induction which has not celebrated professional learning.**
- **Policy documents at national level have not been clear about the nature of progression in learning to teach from ITT to induction.**
- **Research into learning to teach has not been well used in terms of impact on policy.**

Will the current changes in national induction policy lead to effective practice in induction?

So far this chapter has established three things; firstly *that* effective induction practice has been elusive; secondly, *ways* in which effective induction practice has been elusive (links to initial teacher training, lack of systematic support and inconsistencies of provision); thirdly, *why* effective induction practice has been difficult. I want to move on now to consider the potential of the current induction arrangements in addressing some of the difficulties in the past. Will *your* experience as an NQT be different from your predecessors'?

I believe that the short answer to this question is generally 'yes', and I also believe that this is due to major changes in the culture and context of both initial teacher training and schools.

Of critical importance here is the development of the role of the mentor. This was conceived in the James Report (1972) and through the development of partnerships in ITT instigated in Circulars 9/92 (DFE 1992) and 14/93 (DFE 1993) (which set out the national framework at the time for primary and secondary teacher training) has now become firmly established in schools. The principles behind these Circulars were significant in so far as they shifted the focus of control for ITT from the colleges and universities to the schools. A central element of these reforms was the inauguration of mentoring in ITT and the development of mentor training programmes such that schools adopted a formal role in the supervision and assessment of trainee teachers. There followed the widespread and rapid development of partnership schemes in ITT such as those reported by Simco and Sixsmith (1994) and the Oxford intern scheme (Hagger *et al.* 1993). The context for induction is hence different and more positive as through the ITT reforms, many schools will have substantial experience of mentoring. Notwithstanding this, it also needs to be recognised that schools who have not been involved in ITT partnerships will not have this background and the differences in mentoring in ITT and NQT contexts need to be recognised and acknowledged (Moyles *et al.* 1999). There is an emerging national picture of a growing number of schools with trained mentors who have the professional skills and knowledge to enable professional development for beginning teachers, provide effective, individual support and conduct valid and reliable assessments of NQTs' classroom performance. This reality is further strengthened by developments in school culture involving more observation of classroom practice, the enhanced role of accountability and the advent of performance culture.

It is in these ways that the notion of the mentor is significant, because the context of induction policy is different from that experienced at other times. At the time of McNair and James, partnerships between ITT providers and schools did not exist in the way that they do now and there was no detailed understanding of the impact of interaction between school-based tutors/class teachers and beginning teachers on professional development and the assessment of competence. It seems therefore that the current context is fruitful even when compared with the early 1990s in terms of enabling effective induction practice to be developed. The question which remains is whether the new arrangements for induction have the potential to be equally fruitful.

It has already been established that the essence of the new arrangements is to 'combine two interrelated and equally important aspects: an individualised programme of monitoring and support and an assessment of NQTs' performance' (TTA 1999a, p. 3). Looking first at the individualised programme, this centres on the Career Entry and Development Profile (CEDP) which is completed by yourself at the end of a period of initial training and then is followed through in the induction year as targets are set and reviewed with you. The concept of the CEDP addresses at first glance some of the Tickle (1994) concerns which are noted above. It creates a framework for a national system of professional development in induction. The CEDP is centred on individuals' skills and attributes. If used to its full potential, individually tailored induction programmes can be developed and implemented using previously identified strengths, weaknesses and targets as a starting point. This ensures linkage to ITT and provides a sense of direction. There is some evidence to suggest that the general concept of a Career Entry Profile is beginning to influence the quality of induction (Simco and Sixsmith 1999, TTA 1999b), but it is also apparent that this may have limitations if the complexity of learning how to teach and the demands of the induction period are underestimated.

Here I believe that while specific research findings have informed the recent changes to induction, (e.g. Bolam *et al.* 1995), there is a general and constant underestimation by policy-makers of the demands of teaching (Calderhead and Robson 1991, Calderhead 1991, Calderhead and Shorrock 1997). These authors describe some of those demands. Calderhead and Lambert, for example, assert that

> Classrooms are complex and busy places. Faced with 30 or so pupils, teachers encounter competing demands upon their time. Often the situations they confront require immediate responses, and the outcomes of their actions are inevitably associated with a degree of uncertainty. In this environment, the teacher is also constantly visible to pupils and evaluated by them, and the actions teachers take can form precedents, contributing to the norms that form the basis for the future routines and patterns of classroom interaction.
> (Calderhead and Lambert 1992, p. 6)

This kind of analysis becomes all the more profound when it is placed alongside Doyle's (1986) analysis of the nature of classrooms which demonstrates a rich complex social context where teacher and pupil actions and interactions have multiple and simultaneous consequences for all classrooms participants. Calderhead (1991) suggests that the process of learning to teach is fundamentally different from other forms of adult learning because it involves being able to interpret and respond rapidly to classroom environments. Faced with this kind of complexity, it is perhaps little wonder that the instinct for survival and the search for immediate solutions may become more dominant than considered reflection of classroom circumstance.

It also means that as Calderhead and Shorrock (1997) suggest, professional develop-ment will be slow. Technical skills such as the provision of lessons with clear structure, clear pace, the use of appropriate vocabulary, the deployment of carefully selected questions and clear non-verbal communication (Wragg 1993, Wragg and Brown 1993, Simco 1997) become problematic when they are considered within the context of complex classroom environments. The need, for example, to simultaneously pace a lesson at the correct pitch for the majority of pupils but also to ensure that the pace is suitable for more able and less able pupils is difficult to achieve in a classroom environ-ment where there are multiple consequences from single actions. Technical skill in teaching demands a conceptual understanding of teaching and learning processes.

The kinds of monitoring and support envisaged in the new arrangements need to take account of the realities of the induction year and if they are to have impact there needs to be an understanding of the demands and pressures which are experienced by many new teachers. There needs to be an acknowledgement of the rate of professional development. This will mean that the mentoring processes behind the CEDP will be different at different stages of the year. At first there may be quick, pragmatic solu-tions to classroom occurrences. There may be a period of reaction to classroom events which may be difficult to organise into even short-term targets, because the 'issues for survival' may change constantly. Following this, patterns of classroom events may be established (such as behaviour management difficulties with a particular class) and short-term targets can be negotiated in relation to technical skills using the CEDP. It follows that proactive challenges to the assumptions which NQTs may hold about teaching and learning should only occur at a late stage, perhaps even in a second-year CEDP.

There is evidence, then, to suggest that professional development in the early stages of teaching is more complex than is frequently accepted and indeed it may be that as an NQT you are simply overwhelmed by the demands which are made on you and your time. The reality may be that your instinctive priority is to pass the induction year and that longer term professional development is simply not on your agenda. However, it appears that the arrangements for induction begin to take into account the complex-ity and pace of learning to teach. In their evaluation of the pilot of the then new arrangements, the TTA makes the point that good practice is represented through a distinction between short-, medium- and long-term targets (TTA 1999b). Different kinds of targets are relevant to different stages of the induction year and here there is an implicit recognition that professional development is a slow process with different priorities at different times.

The second central element of the induction arrangements is the structured assess-ment of NQTs' performance against the consistent meeting of the standards for the award of Qualified Teacher Status and the induction standards. As with the definition of paths of professional development through the CEDP, I believe that this aspect of the new initiatives has the potential to begin to bridge the gulfs between policy and practice in induction and between ITT and induction. For the first time, there is an explicit separation of professional development and assessment of competence. The professional objectives, goals and aspirations set in the CEDP are not the criteria for assessment as these are represented by the nationally defined standards. There is also a developing culture whereby ITT partnership schools are becoming used to using these in the summative assessment of trainee teachers at the end of a course of teacher training. There will need to be a recognition that the assessment processes in the induction year are different from those in initial training, but the principle of assessment of competence against national standards is becoming established in a way that has not been apparent to the same degree of specificity before.

In conclusion, I would like to return to my earlier claim that the new induction arrangements have the potential to create a much more positive experience of induction than ever before. Bolam *et al.* (1995) raised five issues which needed to be addressed to ensure, from their perspective, that induction policy and practice develops. Current national policy addresses at least partly all of these.

- **National support materials are in the process of being developed by the TTA so that schools have access to strategies to strengthen their induction provision.**
- **The assessment arrangements for NQTs are structured at national level in a way and to an extent that has not happened before.**
- **A Professional Development Profile, the CEDP, has been developed and is now available to all leavers from the ITT providers.**
- **Identification of induction needs for individual NQTs is now embedded within the CEDP and the process of being awarded QTS.**
- **NQTs who are employed on temporary, short-term or supply bases have explicit entitlements and responsibilities.**

Within all of this there will be ongoing issues to raise such as the validity and reliability of assessment of NQTs, the linkage between assessment and professional development and the issue of consistency of provision, but fundamentally the current arrangements address many of the issues which appeared to be compromising earlier attempts at creating effective linkage between policy and practice in induction. More widely, some of the elements of the Tickle analysis are addressed, at least partly. The current initiatives begin to reflect a concept of professional learning while the detail of the strategy has been carefully constructed. Put together with a climate of mentoring and ITT partnership, it seems that current policy has the potential to achieve a high quality induction experience, and early experiences provide some evidence that this is occurring. Interim findings from a survey of NQTs carried out by the Association of Teachers and Lecturers indicated broad satisfaction with mentoring in the induction period, although a previous survey undertaken by the Institute of Education indicated a lower level of satisfaction with many NQTs not experiencing a reduced timetable and high quality mentoring (*Times Educational Supplement*, 18 February 2000).
A major DfES funded research project (Totterdell et al 2002) has provided the first large-scale evidence regarding the extent to which the potential of the induction year has been realised. It paints a mixed picture, suggesting for example that whilst the majority of schools provide support that is both consistent and individualised, a significant number of NQTs are receiving less than their entitlement and the original

Career Entry Profile (CEP) is not being implemented as intended and is seen by many as unsatisfactory. Classroom observation is seen as being particularly beneficial by NQTs.

In the longer term whatever the detail of policy initiatives it is clearly a national aspiration that the kind of situation outlined by Carre (1993) becomes the very rare exception. 'Anthony felt exhausted and stressed at the end of the first week. On the first day he realised that his efforts of planning and collecting resources had been in vain. Not only had the school not communicated the topic he was to teach, but he had no general school information, school policies or curriculum outlines. ... Feedback about his performance was minimal; his facade of confidence made people reticent to help' (p. 209). It will be interesting to consider whether indeed this is the case and whether the new induction arrangements do transform beginning teachers' experience of the first year of teaching.

Chapter 2:
Preparing Yourself for
the Induction Period

 **SIGNPOST** In this chapter you will find information about:

- **how to complete the first two sections of the Career Entry and Development Profile;**
- **the kinds of things you can do prior to your induction period to help you prepare effectively.**

Introduction and chapter overview

It may be that you are reading this book prior to the start of your induction period and it is hoped that this chapter will provide you with some strategies for preparing you for the year. Indeed, the whole idea behind the induction arrangements is to create a seamlessness between ITT and induction such that the transition between the two is as smooth as possible. The key document in this process is the Career Entry and Development Profile. This is a formal statutory document and you will need to consider carefully the approach you will take to its completion. The Career Entry and Development Profile is a document that all newly qualified teachers in England are required to complete. It was first introduced by the Teacher Training Agency in May 1998 and the 2003 version contains major revisions. Its main purposes are:

- *To ensure that all NQTs have an individual path of professional development* **which takes account of strengths and weaknesses as measured against the standards for the award of QTS. This is a really important element of the induction period arrangements because it states that what really matters is an action plan in relation to you as an individual and it follows that your experience of the induction period may well be very different from other NQTs in your school.**

- *To ensure that ITT and Continuing Professional Development are seamless.* **This is alluded to above, but here the point is that your professional development in the induction period bears some relation to the characteristics of your practice prior to qualification. I argued in Chapter I that this notion of seamlessness has been notoriously difficult to achieve over the last seventy years or so. It may well be that the CEDP is an effective strategy in making progress in this difficult area.**

- *To ensure that monitoring and support are effective.* **This is a third purpose of the CEDP. Because it is a formal statutory document, it should mean that you leave ITT with a very clear idea of your specific strengths and areas for development. It 'forces' you to engage in dialogue with tutors and mentors about these. In school the document creates a situation where you have to work out an** individual programme of professional development which is supported and monitored by your induction tutor's actions. Used effectively the CEDP both focuses your professional reflection and guides this through collaborative discussions.

I believe that if you use the CEDP properly, it is a key way to ensure that you have a really effective experience of the induction period, in which you gain a sense of achievement as you make progress against specific individual professional objectives. It is also important to note at this point that the CEDP is not tied in with the assessment of the induction period. While the objectives which you set will be reviewed as part of the formal review meeting, the CEDP will not be used formally to assess the induction period. In this respect in order to pass the induction period you need to fulfil the requirements relating to the consistent meeting of the standards for the award of QTS and the induction standards (see Chapter 4). The meeting of the objectives in your action plan is a separate but related issue.

To enable the purposes noted above to be met the CEDP has three main parts:

- **You are required to complete transition point one prior to leaving initial teacher training. Part one of this section includes basic biographical information and some outline details of your course of ITT. You are also required to outline key strengths and priorities for further professional development. This section requires considerable thought because what you write here will relate closely to your path of professional development during the induction year itself.**

- **Transition point two is completed at the beginning of the induction period after you have left ITT. It consists of an action plan for your professional development that you have negotiated with your induction tutor in school and focuses on specific objectives which have been agreed between you and your school.**

- **Transition point three occurs at the end of the induction year where there is an opportunity for you and your induction tutor to review your progress over the whole of the induction period and plan for the next phase of your professional deelopment.**

This chapter is concerned with providing you with some support as you complete transition point one of the CEDP, while Chapter 3 is devoted to issues surrounding transition point two of the CEDP. The format of transition point one can be seen in Figures I and 2, while the format of transition point two is on page 40 of Chapter 3. At this point, particularly if you have not met the CEDP before, you may wish to familiarise yourself with these three figures so that you can get a feel for the document as a whole.

There will be two sections to this chapter:

- **Section One focuses on the Career Entry and Development Profile, particularly that part of it which is completed before you leave Initial Teacher Training.**

- **SectionTwo considers the kinds of activity with which you may wish to engage prior to the start of the induction year itself.**

Section One

Completing transition point one of the CEDP before you leave Initial Teacher Training

Before you complete transition point one of the CEDP, you will need to undertake some preparation to ensure that what you write in these sections is appropriate. The analytical part of this in particular is dependent on some careful thought as it needs to reflect the reality of your recognised strengths and weaknesses. Although the document is in one sense very straightforward, it needs to be completed with the same care as you would a letter of application to a school; every word counts! It also needs to be reflective of all the work you will have carried out in ITT to measure your progress towards the standards for the award of QTS. In other words, it needs to be evidence based.

What is the evidence base for completing transition point one of the CEDP?

The detail of this will vary according to how your ITT provider has handled the tracking of the standards for the award of QTS, but you will need to ensure that at least some of the following are used in the completion this section.

- *Final placement report.* This is probably the single most important piece of evidence, and because it is likely in many cases that this will have been used to construct a reference for your first post, it is necessary for there to be a resemblance between what you consider to be your strengths and priorities for development and what is written on your final placement report. Many ITT providers use reports which are structured according to the standards for the award of QTS and which contain a section which identifies areas of strength and priorities for further professional development. An excerpt from such a report proforma is included in Figure 3 (pages 24–27).

- *Final placement files.* It may be worthwhile to revisit your final placement files containing planning, evaluation and records of your assessment of children's learning as you identify the detail of strengths and priorities for development.

- *Other placement reports.* You may wish to cite evidence from placement reports, other than a final placement report, particularly where there is evidence that a particular strength has been consistently apparent in your training.

- *Profiles measuring your progress towards the standards.* You may well be aware that many ITT providers require trainees to audit their progress towards the standards for the award of QTS using a profile which lists the standards, and requires them to provide evidence in relation to the achievement of either groups of standards or individual standards. Indeed, it may be the case that you already have a portfolio of sample evidence relating to the standards you have met at various stages in your course.

- *Records of objective-setting proformas.* Many ITT providers encourage trainees to target-set in various ways on formal block placements. This process typically involves trainees identifying objectives, devising action and ensuring that success criteria are defined. The proforma in Figure 4 (page 28) is used by one ITT

Summary of your initial teacher training

|_____

Training provider/recommending body

|_____

Title of ITT programme

|_____

Length of programme in years and months

|_____

Is your training full time or part time?

|_____

Date of successful programme completion

| ☐ ☐ ☐ ☐ ☐ ☐

Age range(s)   Foundation   Key Stage 1   Key Stage 2   Key Stage 3   Key Stage 4   16-19
covered   Stage

|_____

Specialist subject(s), if applicable

|_____

Other information about the teacher training programme[1]

[1] For example: distinctive features of training and/or school experience; additional qualifications during the course; coverage of non-core subjects; details of school placements – eg. year groups and subject(s) taught.

Figure I. Transition point one of the Career Entry and Development Profile (TTA, 2003a).

Transition point one – reflecting with your tutor on your professional development

The notes page opposite provides space for you to make annotations that will act as an aide-memoire to your thinking. Alternatively, you may wish to write more extensively in response to the questions. You are encouraged to choose your own format or to select and/or adapt a format from the supplementary materials available to support the CEDP. The following questions are not an exhaustive list; you can, of course, add your own.

1 At this stage, which aspect(s) of teaching do you find most interesting and rewarding? **What has led to your interest in these areas?**

How would you like to develop these interests?

2 As you approach the award of QTS, what do you consider to be your main strengths and achievements as a teacher? **Why do you think this?**

What examples do you have of your achievements in these areas?

3 In which aspects of teaching would you value further experience in the future? **For example:**

- aspects of teaching about which you feel less confident, or where you have had limited opportunities to gain experience;

- areas of particular strength or interest on which you want to build further.

At the moment, which of these areas do you particularly hope to develop during your induction period?

4 As you look ahead to your career in teaching, you may be thinking about your longer-term professional aspirations and goals. Do you have any thoughts at this stage about how you would like to see your career develop?

Figure 2. Transition point one of the Career Entry and Development Profile (TTA, 2003a).

Transition point one   Date:

Note down your response to the questions, where you might find evidence to support your thinking, and/or the reasoning that led you to this response:

Summary check -- How well have you:
- reflected on your broader experience and the relevant skills and expertise you have developed?
- thought about why you are particularly motivated towards some particular aspects of teaching?
- identified why you want to find out more about, or gain more experience and expertise in, some areas of teaching?

Figure 2 (continued). Transition point one of the Career Entry and Development Profile.

SUMMATIVE REPORT TO BE USED ON ALL BLOCK PLACEMENTS
WHERE THE REPORT DOUBLES AS A REFERENCE ENTRY FOR THE TRAINEE

FINAL BLOCK PLACEMENT REPORT

WRITTEN BY THE ASSOCIATE TUTOR (OR SUPERVISOR) AND RETURNED TO THE
PARTNERSHIP OFFICE

Comments made on this form are used as part of the College reference for students

COURSE _____

TRAINEE _____ AGE RANGE TAUGHT _____

SCHOOL _____ NO. OF CHILDREN IN CLASS _____

LINK TUTOR _____ ASSOCIATE TUTOR _____

DATES OF PLACEMENT _____ CLASS TEACHER _____

_____ (if different)

_____

CONTEXT SPECIFIC INFORMATION
[Please give some relevant background about the context in which this Block Placement occurred (e.g. the age range of the class, locality and type of school: any particular difficulties or constraints the trainee encountered).]

[Insert first name of trainee] .... carried out their final block placement in

PROFESSIONALISM (Standards Section 1)
[Please comment on the trainee's ability to form effective working relationships with colleagues, to be an appropriate role model for pupils, contribute to the general life of the school and convey enthusiasm and imagination.]

Whilst on the placement .... showed a range of general professional qualities. She / he

Proforma Doc 2   Page 1 of 4

Figure 3. Example of a final block placement report proforma.

SUBJECT KNOWLEDGE AND APPLICATION (Standards Section 2)
[Please comment on the knowledge and understanding which the trainee has of the National Curriculum as a whole, including the Early Years curriculum if appropriate.]

....

[Please comment, under the subject headings below, on the trainee's knowledge and understanding of the subject, of the National Curriculum Programmes of Study / Early Years curriculum and on their ability to cope securely with subject-related questions from pupils.]

ENGLISH
In English .... demonstrated that

MATHEMATICS
In mathematics he / she

SCIENCE
In science he / she

ICT
In ICT he / she

RE
In RE he / she

SPECIALIST SUBJECT
In his / her specialist subject [name subject] ....

continued overleaf

Figure 3 (continued). Example of a final block placement report proforma.

FOUNDATION SUBJECTS (as appropriate)
In the broader curriculum .... showed the following areas to be particular strengths:

PLANNING, TEACHING AND CLASS MANAGEMENT (Standards Sections 3.1 & 3.3)

PLANNING
[Please comment on the trainee's ability to prepare medium-term plans and lesson plans which reflect the National Curriculum Programmes of Study, or the curriculum for under-fives if appropriate, have clear DLOs, and plan for progression and make cross-curricular links.]

In his / her planning both before and during the placement .... demonstrated

TEACHING AND CLASS MANAGEMENT
[Please comment, with reference to specific subjects, on the extent to which the trainee used different forms of classroom organisation effectively, set high expectations for pupils, managed children's behaviour well, used stimulating teaching methods, including clear explanations and effective questioning, met individual differences, and managed the work of others in the classroom, as appropriate.]

.... showed competence in the following aspects of teaching strategies:

MONITORING AND ASSESSMENT
(Standards Section 3.2)
[Please comment on the trainee's ability to identify and assess relevant individual differences between pupils using a range of techniques, use assessments to inform day-to-day planning, provide appropriate feedback to pupils, keep whole class records, and report to parents.]

In terms of the assessment and recording of pupils' progress ....

Figure 3 (continued). Example of a final block placement report proforma.

IDENTIFICATION OF STRENGTHS AND PRIORITIES FOR FURTHER DEVELOPMENT
(for possible inclusion in the Career Entry and Development Profile or Target Setting for future placements as appropriate).
[Please identify up to four strengths and four priorities for development in relation to the trainee's teaching.]

The following have been identified as particular strengths and areas for further development:

HEADTEACHER'S COMMENTS

Signature of headteacher ....

Number of absences from the placement ....

OVERALL RECOMMENDATION

Pass

Fail

Deferred assessment. This category is only to be used in exceptional circumstances relating to illness, personal difficulty or other unavoidable constraints.

Signature of trainee (who should be provided with a copy of the report) ....

Signature of associate tutor ....

Date ....

Proforma Doc 2   Page 4 of 4

Figure 3 (continued). Example of a final block placement report proforma.

PROFESSIONAL OBJECITVE-SETTING PROFORMA

AREAS OF STRENGTH	PRIORITIES FOR FURTHER DEVELOPMENT
1.	1.
2.	2.

OBJECTIVES AND ACTION PLAN FOR _____ state period of time which is covered by the action plan

OBJECTIVES	STANDARD (state which standard is being covered in the objective)	ACTIONS TO BE TAKEN	SUCCESS CRITERIA How will you know it's been achieved ?	RESOURCES	TARGET DATE FOR ACHIEVEMENT	REVIEW OF OBJECTIVE
1.						
2.						
3.						
4.						

Figure 4. Example of objective-setting proforma used in ITT.

provider. It can be used as evidence for identifying strengths and priorities because it will expose areas of the standards which have been met well and also those where there is still a priority to address.

- *Course assignments.* It may well be that certain specific assignments have been related explicitly to certain of the standards for the award of QTS and it is possible that you could then cite these assignments as evidence that you have met a specific requirement.

- *Subject audits.* You may recall that Standard 2.1 of the Standards for QTS states that candidates have to demonstrate a secure knowledge and understanding of the subject(s) they are trained to teach. For those qualifying to teach secondary pupils this knowledge and understanding should be at a standard equivalent to degree level.

(DfES/TTA 2002 p. 7)

Many providers provide trainees with a document which enables them to audit the subject knowledge requirements and it may be that there are areas here where, while you have achieved the standards, you will feel less than strong.

What is the general process of completing transition point one of the CEDP?

There is obviously no one way of completing the initial stages of the CEDP because the arrangements will vary provider by provider, but I hope that the following illustrations will provide you with examples of how this process is undertaken and that this may be of some help as you anticipate the completion of transition point one. One main difference between the two models is that the first involves school and college personnel working in an integrated fashion, with the major emphasis on the college tutorials, while the second is much more strongly school oriented. Both approaches have a strong element of completing the CEDP in the light of various different kinds of evidence.

Provider X (**primary undergraduate**) asks trainees to complete an objective-setting proforma prior to final block placement. This is discussed with a college tutor and is then reviewed at an interim stage of the placement by the school-based mentor where fresh objectives are established with the trainee. The summative report on the placement is prepared and this identifies strengths and areas for development for possible inclusion in the CEDP. Back at the college, there is a conference week which focuses on the induction period, its nature and requirements. As part of this all trainees have an extended tutorial with a college tutor which considers the final summative report and a range of other evidence in the completion of transition point one of the CEDP. The trainee then prepares the document in rough and the college tutor provides further comments before it is submitted formally.

Provider Y (secondary PGCE) asks trainees to complete a profile which demonstrates how they are meeting the standards for the award of QTS. This is built up gradually as the year progresses and there is a focus on different standards on different placements. There is also a requirement for a portfolio of evidence from school and college-based elements of the course which provides evidence in relation to groups of standards. Towards the end of the final period of school based work, there is a three-way meeting in school between the school mentor, the trainee and the university tutor at which there is a discussion about the extent to which the standards have been met, and evidence for this is cited. Transition point one of the CEDP is completed in draft at this meeting. The trainee then submits this to the mentor who checks that it has been completed satisfactorily and the document is finally signed off by the university tutor.

Completing the 'summary of your initial teacher training' sub-section

Much of this section of the CEDP is fairly self-explanatory, and indeed in some ITT providers, trainees are provided with a printed version of the main elements of this section. Some thought, however, needs to be given to the part entitled 'Other infor-maiton about the teacher training programme', and here it is good to include something wherever possible rather than leave the section blank. In regard to 'other information about the initial teacher training programme', the following illustrations may trigger your thinking about the kinds of things you could include:

- (*Primary*) **During the course of my training, I undertook a one-week intensive placement in an inner city primary school where a large group of trainees worked on a school-share programme with school staff. This involved groups of four trainees working in every classroom in the school with school staff acting as mentors.**

- (*Secondary*) **Although my course focused on my subject specialism, English, I have had the formal opportunity to observe teaching in the RE and History departments at one of my placement schools and to take part in the teaching of small groups of pupils.**

- (*Early Years*) **A formal part of the course involved my developing an appreciation of the interplay between health and education in the provision for under fives.**

- (*Secondary*) **As part of my course I attended a junior school so that I could develop my understanding of key stage 2/3 transition.**

- (*Primary*) **As part of my PE subject specialism, I was able to elect for a module entitled 'Outdoor Education in the Primary School'. This was invaluable in giving me some basic understanding of the potential of outdoor education. It is certainly an area which I would like to follow through.**

You may also want to include experience gained outside the course, for example:

- **part-time jobs which are with young people, such as summer playschemes;**

- **involvement in sports activities with children;**

- skills related to those needed for teaching, but gained in another profession or job;

- involvement in a school **PTA**;

- parental help in a classroom, or voluntary work in a school prior to or during training;

- being a parent governor.

Completing transition point one – Reflecting with your tutor on your professional development

This section asks four key questions:

- **At this stage which aspect(s) of teaching do you find most interesting and rewarding?**
- **As you approach the award of QTS, what do you consider to be your main strengths and achievements as a teacher?**
- **In which aspects of teaching would you value further experience in the future?**
- **As you look ahead to your career in teaching you may be thinking about your longer-term professional aspirations and goals. Do you have any thoughts at this stage about how you would like to see your career develop?**

(TTA 2003a p. 12)

When responding to these questions you are encouraged to choose a format and approach that matches your style and needs. In general I would suggest an approach that encourages depth and precision as the discussions you will have at this stage will potentially influence the whole of your induction period. Questions two and three in particular demand considerable skill and challenge you to be precise about strengths and further experience.

You need to consider a number of issues as you decide what to include. In terms of which strengths to include:

- **I think that it is generally good practice for you to include a range of statements from the different areas of the QTS standards. This means you need to include a breadth of strengths from:**
  - **professional values and practice**
  - **subject knowledge**
  - **teaching.**
- **It is probably easiest to include items from teaching as this area is the most extensive and includes critical areas such as planning and assessment. However, I think you should be aware of strengths in relation to other areas of the standards and ensure that these are properly included so that there is a proper balance.**
- **In my view each statement should be written as a formal sentence. The statement may relate to an individual standard, or it may relate to a group of standards. However, whatever the case, it does need to be written in a way that**

reflects your practice. It is not merely a case of paraphrasing, or even worse copying out the standards. The whole point of the document is that it is a reflection of you as an individual, and it will be the case that the way in which the document is written will differ from person to person. However, you may wish to show how your own individual statements relate to specific standards. You may wish to put the code for a standard – say 2.1 – after your statement. I do not think there is any point in writing out the whole of the standard.

- If you are claiming that a particular area is a strength then say so with clarity and conviction. The points which you have identified are the areas which represent the most positive aspects of your practice so do use phrases such as 'very good', 'able to…', 'excellent at…'.

- The strengths you do cite need to link with what is said in supporting evidence. In particular the final placement report will have identified certain strengths which need to be in evidence in the strengths which you list.

- I think that you need to be as precise as possible in your language. If you say that 'I feel that I have a major strength in differentiation in literacy', this says relatively little and so will be less useful in ensuring that objectives at transition point two are precisely related to what you have written at transition point one. If you write 'During the course of my final block placement, I became particularly adept at meeting individual children's needs through my provision for independent group work in the literacy hour', you are conveying a much more precise concept of your particular strength in this area.

Many of the above points will also apply to defining aspects of teaching that you would value further experience of in the future, but there are also some particular issues about which you should be aware as you complete this section:

- The assumption is that you have met the standards for the award of QTS. Therefore you need to phrase your priorities for further professional development in such a way that is indicative of this. You do not want to give an impression that there are important areas where you have major weaknesses. I suggest that one key phrase may be 'Building on my achievements in initial teacher training, I wish to…'.

- You may also wish to be careful about the areas from which you select your priorities for further development. In primary, for example, you may be more aware of priorities for development in the CORE subjects because these have had a higher profile in your ITT course. While you may well wish to include elements of these in one or more of your statements, it would not be good to convey an impression that all your priorities are within the CORE.

I think that it is appropriate for at least one of your priorities to build on your strengths. For example if one of your strengths is the provision of very well structured introductory explanations, you may wish to extend this to the plenary of your lessons where you feel that there is a certain lack of structure and cohesion.

I hope that through reading the above you understand more clearly some of the main issues as you put together transition point one of your CEDP. In order to help this process further, you will see that I now include two examples of records relating to transition point one which show different approaches to writing the document. The first example (Figure 5) is written by a primary trainee, Richard, at the end of the course of initial teacher training. It shows an effective approach to preparing the CEDP and takes account of many of the points noted above. Most of the statements are precise. In the section on strengths, the general approach is to use a broad statement and then to elaborate this using a specific example. Science specialist knowledge is a strength, but in particular Richard feels able to teach through experimental and investigative approaches. In areas for development, Richard begins each one with a statement about what he has achieved during initial training and then focuses on a specific area where there is a need for further development. He is careful to avoid giving any indication that he has not met any of the standards. You will notice that following each statement there is a code which shows how this statement relates to the standards. He is hence able to demonstrate that while the statements have been written using his own words they do relate closely to the standards for the award of QTS. In the last area for professional development, you can see that Richard has selected an area which relates to his subject specialism in science. He has a strength in science and plans to develop his understanding of the role of the science co-ordinator during the induction period.

Transition point one

What do you consider to be your main strengths and achivements as a teacher?

1. I have strengths in planning to achieve progression in pupils' learning in the short, medium and long term. I am particularly strong in my planning for the literacy hour and am able here to include very well focused learning objectives and opportunities for assessment. (3.1.1)

2. I have a strong capability in science, my specialist area of training. This is reflected in background knowledge of the subject, my lesson planning and methods of assessment. I demonstrate effective use of resources and am particularly able to integrate AT1 in my teaching. Indeed experimental and investigative science is a real strength. (2.16)

3. I have strengths in the following aspects of teaching and classroom management:

    - Setting the highest of expectations of pupil behaviour in the classroom. Here I am well able to anticipate potentially difficult situations and can put in place strategies to avoid them. (3.2.1)
    - Provide clear, purposeful well paced instructions to the children. Lesson introductions are a particular strength. (3.3.3)

4. A key part of my final placement was managing the work of the nursery nurse attached to the reception unit. I developed a strength in this area and I built a very effective working relationship for mutual benefit. (1.6)

Figure 5. Richard's Career Entry and Development Profile, section B (final version).

Transition point one
_____

In which aspects of teaching would you value further experience in the future?

1   Building on my understanding of approaches to assessment in the primary classroom, I wish to consolidate strategies in assessment, particularly in regard to setting individual targets for pupils in numeracy. (3.2.6)

2   I have a secure understanding of lesson planning. In the induction period I wish to consider the area of planning for differentiation in more depth, in particular planning so that I differentiate in a variety of ways. (3.3.4)

3   I am able to teach using well paced and structured introductions. I wish to focus further on my use of voice (level and tone) in order to ensure that all children remain motivated and stimulated through my teaching. (3.3.1)

4   A major strength is the teaching of science and in the College course there was a module on the role of the science co-ordinator. In my induction period I wish to put into practice the skills which I developed through that course, perhaps in shadowing a science co-ordinator. (1.5)

Figure 5 (continued). Richard's Career Entry and Development Profile, section B (final version).

Further, in his discussion with his college tutor, Richard confirmed a real commitment to and interest in science and this arose out of a consideration of the first question. He wanted to signal this interest in the identification of science as a particular strength. Additionally and in connection with question four, Richard wanted to note his long-term commitment to the subject and his aspiration of becoming a science co-ordinator. Overall Richard's strategy was to focus his thinking on questions two and three, but to incorporate wider questions into this reponse.

I have chosen a second example which was written part-way through the process of considering transition point one. In Collette's secondary ITT course, the trainees have to draft an initial reponse prior to discussing this with the school-based mentor and writing up the document formally. The draft version which Collette prepared can be seen in Figure 6. In the tutorial following the submission of the CEDP, Collette was given some advice about how to improve her CEDP. In response to the question about strengths, Collette had proposed a number of areas which were related to various different areas of the QTS standards. She was encouraged to show how these statements related to individual standards. Some of the statements demonstrated her belief that she had a particular strength in an area. Number 4, for example, starts with the phrase 'I am particularly strong'. However, other statements are less secure – number 2 is perhaps an underestimation of Collette's ability in this area. The phrase 'I believe that many of my key learning objectives…' suggests a degree of uncertainty and also implies that this strength is not consistent. Some of the priorities for further professional development lack detail and Collette was advised to ensure that a sentence providing some further detail be included. Under number 4, the tutor wished to know what Collette actually meant by 'a wider range of approaches'. Collette is also in danger of giving an impression that she has not met the QTS standards. Like many trainees, she has little experience of preparing reports for parents, but she does have some knowledge about the process gained through a school-based seminar on the course and her tutor encourages her to stress what has occurred, rather than emphasising what has not. Following the tutorial, Collette took this advice and developed a much more precise and upbeat version of her record of transition point one, but one which did still, accurately and honestly, reflect her strengths and areas for development.

Transition point one

What do you consider to be your main strengths and achievements as a teacher?

1   I have a secure knowledge of most of the concepts and skills in the teaching of my specialist subject, and have a particular strength in the teaching of physical geography.

2   I believe that many of my key learning objectives are clear, and that I am able to set tasks which lead to high levels of pupil motivation.

3   I am committed to ensuring that all individual pupils reach their potential.

4   I am particularly strong at providing constructive written feedback to pupils and believe there is evidence that pupils have acted on this feedback in their future work.

Figure 6. Collette's Career Entry and Development Profile, section B (draft version).

Anticipating the induction period

The aim of this section is to help you structure your thoughts as you prepare for the induction period. It is not concerned with the detail of setting up your classroom or approaches to finding your way around the department, because you will be involved with these things as a matter of course. It is much more about encouraging you to anticipate the characteristics of the induction period, because this will be the key to your professional development in the year.

I think that a very important part of your preparation should be your understanding of key roles and responsibilities in the induction period. This clarity should help your induction period get off to a good start because you will be able to understand the role of all colleagues. Some of these responsibilities are laid down in the DfES guidance, particularly those related to assessment, and are effectively statutory, while with others there is more scope for interpretation. Clearly the detail of these roles will vary according to whether you are a secondary or primary NQT or whether the school is large or small, but it may be useful to consider now an outline of the kinds of roles which will be central to your experience as an NQT.

What are the key roles and responsibilities in the induction period?

Your role centres on the CEDP which you will need to discuss with your induction tutor at a very early stage in the period, perhaps even before the year begins. While your school should have a clear understanding of its responsibilities towards you as an NQT, you will also have a responsibility to ensure that action agreed in the CEDP is taken forward and achieved and to do this you will need to make sure that you collect sample evidence of your achievements in relation to that action plan and the general requirements of the induction year. You also have a responsibilty to ensure that you select a format for action planning that reflects a considered choice. This book (Chapter 3) provides a resource to help you with this. You may also wish to refer to TTA publications, notably the supplementary support materials associated with the CEDP (TTA 2003b). The onus is in addition on you to ensure that you take responsibility for your own professional development. It is clearly something which cannot be done to you or without your full and active involvement. It is also very important that you raise any concerns about your induction programme at an early stage, because in the very rare instance of anyone being assessed and found not to be meeting the requirements of the induction period, the fact that a difficulty with the programme was not mentioned may be taken into account in any appeal situation. If you are unable or unwilling to raise any concerns in school, you may wish to contact an LEA inspector/adviser or seek advice from a professional association.

The headteacher has two statutory responsibilities. The first is that it is the head who has the lead responsibility for ensuring your assessment against the induction period requirements and communicating a recommendation about your assessment onwards, normally to the LEA. Secondly, the head has responsibility for ensuring that the induction programme is set up and relates to your needs and aspirations. In practice it may well be that this responsibility is delegated to others within the school, particularly the induction tutor who is probably the most significant person in your induction period. The **induction tutor** in this way, then, is the person who will have responsibility on a day-to-day basis for your programme. S/he will also observe you teaching, will hold professional review meetings with you (see Chapter 3) and will also be involved in the formal assessment process (see Chapter 4). In the first few weeks s/he will set up the induction programme with you, perhaps according to a framework set by the headteacher. It may also be the case that the induction tutor will have a role in co-ordinating others who are involved in your professional development programme. The **governing body** of your school also has a role to play in ensuring that it is prepared to take on the responsibility of providing an induction programme and that it plays some part, with the headteacher, in its monitoring and implementation.

The **local education authority** (or equivalent body for independent schools) has key responsibilities in the induction period. They relate to making decisions about the assessment of your induction period on the basis of recommendations from your head-teacher and then communicating this to you, the headteacher of your school, and the General Teaching Council for England. The LEA (or Schools Council Induction Panel for independent schools) also has a key role in quality assurance as it will need to be satisfied that the arrangements which are being made for induction in its schools are satisfactory.

Each of the people and bodies noted above will have a role in ensuring that the start of your induction period is smooth and supportive. You may find it useful to use the following checklist of events which ideally should occur either before or very early on in the induction period.

- **You will need various pieces of *documentation* from school: the staff handbook, information about routines and procedures, medium-term plans, policy documents and so forth. You may feel overwhelmed by the amount of documentation which is given to you and it may make sense for you to ask that the information flow is managed so that you receive only what is essential for the first day or week. Alternatively, your induction tutor may be able to signpost the documentation for you so that you can work your way through it relatively easily.**
- **You need to *show your induction tutor your CEDP* prior to the formal start of term and agree a time very early in the term for you to meet with her/him to establish your first action plan; this will be part of transition point two. In many cases this will occur at an informal meeting prior to the term beginning, and here I believe it is useful for you to ask a number of key questions, particularly in relation to the release time and the key people involved in the arrangements.**

- **At the first meeting in the actual term, I think it is reasonable for you to be presented with *provisional dates for professional review meetings* (Chapter 3) and the formal assessment meeting (Chapter 4) in the first term. You may wish to set a loose agenda for this first meeting at the point where you show your induction tutor your CEDP prior to the start of term.**

- **It is important that prior to the start of term you revisit transition point one of your CEDP that you completed prior to the award of QTS and consider possibilities for your *action plan* at transition point two, now that you have started your induction period. This will ensure some relationship to what you wrote at the end of ITT. I think these possibilities will normally be fairly short term in the first place. You will have a great deal to achieve in the first few weeks of your post, and to have a few, defined objectives, well thought out in advance, can give you a sense of purpose and direction.**

- **As noted above, one of the key elements of the induction period is the *10% release time* and the arrangements for this should be established in principle prior to the start of the induction year.**

Chapter 3:
Effective Support and
Monitoring in the Induction Year

**SIGNPOST** In this chapter you will find material to support you in the following areas:

- **use of the Career Entry and Development Profile during the induction period;**
- **observation of your teaching and the provision of written feedback;**
- **the nature of other professional development activities in the induction period, observation of other teachers, collaborative planning etc.;**
- **the nature of a professional development programme;**
- **what to expect in professional review meetings.**

Introduction and chapter overview

The opening chapter of this book established that the arrangements for the induction period have two central elements, one related to the formal, statutory assessment of the period, the other related to effective support and monitoring. This chapter is concerned with the latter and suggests it is highly important as it is the essence of your *entitlement* as an NQT. A primary purpose of the previous DfEE regulations underpinning induction, Circular 5/99, is to ensure that the kind of situation where there is no or inadequate systematic professional support becomes a thing of the past.

A key paragraph in Circular 5/99 provides us with the rationale behind the notion of effective support in the induction period:

> The induction programme will involve a combination of monitoring, support and assessment which are inter-related. Each component should be addressed early in planning the individual NQT's induction programme to ensure that the NQT is fully supported in meeting the requirements of the induction period and that the assessment is fair.
>
> (DfEE 1999, para. 35)

This principle is carried forward into the new DfES regulations published in 2003.

It is possible to identify certain principles from this statement:

- **You are entitled to a high level of support.**
- **It is not fair to assess how well you have met the requirements of the induction period if you have not been provided with support.**
- **You should have an induction programme which sets out the kind of support which you will experience.**

- You should know about the kind of support you will receive at an early stage in the induction process.

There are four key ways in which these principles can be put into practice, and this chapter is organised according to these key headings:

- Section One considers the use of the *Career Entry and Development Profile* (CEDP) and includes material on the place of setting objectives. The CEDP is a central document in the induction period, because it gives you as **NQT** the opportunity to ensure that the kinds of things you consider to be important are on the agenda.
- Section Two is concerned with the issue of *observation* of and discussion about your teaching. It considers the style of observations, their purpose and foci.
- Section Three documents other elements of *support* which may be available such as your observing other teachers, collaborative teaching and peer support.
- Section Four is about the *professional review meetings* which are an integral part of the induction process. Here their nature, scope and purpose is considered and their relationship with the formal assessment process established.

Using the Career Entry and Development Profile in the induction period

Section One

When you start your induction period you will have completed transition point one of your Career Entry and Development Profile. Chapter 2 provided a general overview to this key document and explored approaches to the completion of these sections. The important point is that you will begin your induction period with a clear statement of your strengths and priorities for development against the standards for the award of Qualified Teacher Status. The purpose of transition point two is to translate strengths and priorities into an effective action plan. Figures 7 and 8 show the key questions in the CEDP at transition point two and, as with transition point one, encourages a range of formats to be used as a response to the questions. In general, the idea is that an action plan is completed at an initial meeting between you and your induction tutor at a very early stage in your induction period. Then, as the induction period progresses, there is a further intention for the plan to be revised and new objectives negotiated as appropriate. The action plan has a number of key elements and each element requires very careful consideration. It is very easy for the action plan process to be a paper exercise and much harder but also much more rewarding for it to be a worthwhile course of professional development. Over the next few pages you will find some detailed guidance about the process of constructing an action plan, arising out of transition point two.

Transition point two – discussing with your induction tutor your priorities for induction and how these relate to, build on, or differ from the priorities you identified at transition point one.

The notes page opposite provides space for you to make annotations that will act as an aide-memoire to your thinking. Alternatively, you may wish to write more extensively in response to the questions. You are encouraged to choose your own format or to select and/or adapt a format from the supplementary materials available to support the CEDP (see page 26). The following questions are not an exhaustive list; you can, of course, add your own.

1 At the moment, what do you consider to be your most important professional development priorities during your induction period?

Why are these issues the most important for you at this time? In thinking about this, consider:

- your responses at transition point one;
- the post in which you are starting your induction period;
- any feedback you have already had from your induction tutor or other colleagues;
- your self review against the QTS and Induction Standards.

2 How have your priorities changed since transition point one?

For example, are there any new needs and areas for development related to:

- the pupils you will be teaching: for example, their attainment levels; the proportion of pupils who are gifted and talented or who have special educational needs; the number of pupils who speak English as an additional language;
- the context of the school: for example, its phase, size, geographical area, organisation;
- the subject(s) and year group(s) you will be teaching[3]
- the courses and schemes of work you will be using;
- the resources to which you will have access to support pupils' learning;
- responsibilities you will be taking on[4]

3 How would you prioritise your needs across your induction period?

What do you feel should be the short-term, medium-term or long-term priorities?

What is your reasoning for prioritising in this way?

4 What preparation, support or development opportunities do you feel would help you move forward with these priorities?

[3] Newly qualified teachers should not normally be required to teach subjects and/or age ranges outside their trained specialisms without the provision of additional support.
[4] Newly qualified teachers should not normally be asked to take on additional non-teaching responsibilities without the provision of additional support.

Figure 7. Transition point two the Career Entry and Development Profile.

Transition point two   Date:

Note down your response to the questions, where you might find evidence to support your thinking, and/or the reasoning that led you to this response:

Summary check – How well have you:

- considered background information about your new school and pupils?
- prepared for your discussions with your induction tutor, deciding how to share your CEDP and other supporting information with them?
- engaged in productive discussion and negotiation with your induction tutor?

Figure 8. Transition point two the Career Entry and Development Profile (cont.).

Setting objectives

This is the key to an effective action plan, in much the same way that effective lesson planning depends on the setting of appropriate lesson objectives. It follows that objectives for your action plan need to be:

- *Related to your stated priorities for development and strengths.* This latter element, building on strengths, is particularly worthwhile to note because valuable objectives can be built on acknowledged strengths.
- *A statement of what the outcome will be* in terms of your own learning, not a description of what you will do.
- *Thoroughly discussed* with your induction tutor.
- *Precise and focused.* This is really important, because it is very difficult to discern progress against broad, unfocused statements.
- *Manageable.* An objective which is very broad in its intent will not lead to *achievable* action. If the objective can't reasonably be achieved, there is little point in noting it down because it will in effect not be actioned.
- *Short, medium or longer term.* In setting the objective you need to be clear whether it can be achieved in a short time period or whether it will take much of the induction period to achieve. If the latter is the case, you will need to be particularly careful that the objective is also focused and precise.
- *Few in number.* If too many are set, their management will become increasingly problematic and any sense of focused professional development will be at considerable risk of not being achieved.

Actions to be taken and by whom

When setting actions it is important that you are clear about the precise nature of the action and who is responsible. Actions should normally be:

- Closely and demonstrably *related* to the agreed objective.
- Stated in such a way that they are an *integral part of the support* offered to you in the induction period. One example of this would be a focused observation in relation to the area of the objective. If this occurs, then the action plan will be 'real' as it will be related to the monitoring of your induction period.
- Have clearly stated *lines of responsibility*, such that you have some responsibility and the induction tutor or other defined colleague also has responsibility.
- Take account of *time constraints*. If they don't they won't be achievable!
- Related to the *resources* column of the action plan. Resources could consist of a number of elements including time, funding, consumables, etc.

Success criteria

The purpose of success criteria is to provide a clear statement of when objectives and defined action have been achieved. It follows that if objectives are precise and focused, it will be relatively straightforward to define success criteria. It will be the case that these relate to both the target date for achievement and also the review date. The latter will be the occasion when the success criteria are considered probably with some sample evidence to judge the extent to which the original objective has been achieved.

The kinds of criteria mentioned under the three headings above are important if action planning is to be effective. I want to move on now to develop a worked example to see how these criteria can work in practice.

Examples of completed action plans arising from transition point two of the Career Entry and Development Profile

The example is taken from a secondary modern foreign-languages NQT, Paula. It is an excerpt from an action plan devised at transition point two (Figure 9) and which was established at the beginning of the academic year. In exploring this example, the following points are apparent:

- **Both objectives are precise and focused. Objective I is concerned, for example, not just with differentiation per se, but with differentiation on a regular basis for mixed ability classes and lower ability sets. It is easy to see what the objective means and that it is achievable. The first objective related very directly to a priority for further development. Both objectives are achievable and realistic and the defined action ensures that there is a way forward in meeting the objective.**

- **Actions are very clearly defined and itemised. In terms of the second objective, the action of becoming familiar with resources to support the GNVQ syllabus is clear and unequivocal. I particularly like the third action under objective one which has a degree of focus. It acknowledges that it will not be possible to develop the objective across all areas of teaching simultaneously, but that there should be a sharp focus on one particular class. This is then carried through very precisely into success criteria and because the action relates to a specific class, it is relatively straightforward to see that this has been achieved.**

- **The target dates for achievement indicate a recognition that some of the actions are short-term, whilst others are medium- and long-term.**

- **The agenda for a review discussion is very clear because the success criteria are very clear. Looking at the second objective, the agenda for the review meeting is defined by three key elements, whether Paula has a 'full understanding' of GNVQ needs, the extent to which she has an increased awareness of appropriate methodology and resources and whether she is in a position to contribute to the GNVQ team. The discussion in the review meeting would need to consider the nature of that full understanding, but the principle of its importance is firmly established.**

All this contrasts somewhat with a second example from Vanessa, a primary NQT. I have selected Vanessa's action plan because it relates to the same area as the secondary NQT example – differentiation. An excerpt from the plan can be seen in Figure 10.

OBJECTIVES	ACTIONS TO BE TAKEN AND BY WHOM	SUCCESS CRITERIA	RESOURCES	TARGET DATE FOR ACHIEVEMENT	REVIEW DATE
1. To differentiate work on a regular basis for pupils, particularly those in mixed ability classes and lower ability sets.	1. To discuss issue fully within Faculty.	1. An ability to work with differentiated materials with specific class.	Department Meeting time	February	} } } March } }
	2. To become fully conversant with Department Resources.	2. An understanding of the Special Needs issues relating to readability etc.	½ day with LSD	Easter	
	3. To work specifically with one class and produce appropriate resources.	3. To be able to produce differentiated materials and share with colleagues.	Link to LSD supported by Head of Faculty		} } } }
	4. To gain greater understanding of Special Needs issues – by link with LSD.	4. Greater skill and confidence in managing differentiation.			} } June } } } }
	5. Plan for work for two topics - Year 8 Link with LSD.	5. More on task activity by students.		May	} } } } }
	6. To share and evaluate resources developed.				
2. To become better acquainted with the GNVQ syllabus.	1. Assistant Head to identify specific training linked to MFL.	1. Full understanding of GNVQ needs.	Training course 1 day ??? ???	February	March
	2. To become better acquainted with Resources.	2. Increased awareness of methodology and resources.	Regular Team meetings.	Ongoing	March
	3. To meet regularly with GNVQ team leader.	3. An ability to contribute to work of GNVQ team.	Needs Analysis following February course.		

Figure 9. Paula's induction year action plan arising from CEDP transition point two.

OBJECTIVES	ACTIONS TO BE TAKEN AND BY WHOM	SUCCESS CRITERIA	RESOURCES	TARGET DATE FOR ACHIEVEMENT	REVIEW DATE
To improve my approach to differentiation	Attend courses, observations and feedback on teaching	Better lesson plans. Evidence of individual children's learning	Observation course Check plans	December	April
To organise and sort through SEN files	Help from CC + head (SENCO) by discussion and leadership	Improved children. Successful working IEPs	Observation Plans	December	April
To improve general termly assessments To implement yearly assessments	discussions with head and school inspector, adviser	Implemented assessments that are being used in planning	School sheets class sheets own sheets discussion	April	June

Figure 10. Vanessa's induction year action plan arising from CEDP transition point two.

There are a number of questions I would need to ask and issues to raise if I was working with Vanessa during her induction period.

- **The objective is very broad and unfocused and it will therefore be difficult to see whether it has been met. In discussion with Vanessa I would want to know if there was a particular subject focus, what she knew about the range of approaches to differentiation and how this objective related to the discussions that occurred at transition point one, completed before she left initial teacher training.**
- **Likewise the actions need considerable elaboration. Observations and feedback on teaching are important but there needs to be a defined focus here based on a specific objective. What will be the focus of the observation? What kinds of feedback will be offered on observed teaching? Will planning be scrutinised to provide a baseline for discussion about differentiation?**

- **There also need to be elaborated statements in relation to the area of 'courses attended', and a clear statement of who is responsible for taking action.**

- **The same kinds of issues can be raised in regard to the proposed success criteria and in addition the relationship between these and the actions and objectives needs further specifying. Both success criteria need elaboration: what does 'better' lesson plans mean? What kind of evidence would be appropriate in terms of individual children's learning?**

The point which I am trying to make here is that the 'devil is in the detail'. The CEDP is a tremendously useful way to give a sense of direction to your professional development in the induction period, but only if the action plan is focused, detailed, manageable and meaningful to your contexts. If these kinds of criteria are not met, then I would argue that the completion of the CEDP is little more than a paper exercise. I would argue also that the professional 'fruits' to be gained from completing it in detail are very considerable.

Section Two

Observing your teaching and the provision of written feedback

There are at least three issues which need to be considered in this section:

- *The content of observation* – when? By whom? With what purpose? Of what?

- *The approach to the observation* – open? Use of prompts? Related to the induction standards?

- *The approach to written feedback* – judgemental? Responsive to your areas of priority? Analytical? Done 'with' you or 'to' you?

The *context* of the observation is important because it gives key messages about its role and status in the induction process. It is important that you are clear about your induction tutor's understanding of the place of observation and there are a number of key questions which you could ask to support this process.

What are the main purposes of observation?

By observation I mean a formal planned occasion when your teaching is observed. Informal observation when an induction tutor or other colleague 'pops in' to a session has its place, but is no substitute for structured observation and analysis of your teaching based on a discussion which recognises your needs and acknowledges your targets. Main purposes include:

- **an opportunity for you to receive feedback in relation to the targets which you have negotiated with your induction tutor through using the Career Entry and Development Profile and to provide a context for review of targets;**

- **an opportunity for you to discuss your progress in the induction period using a specific lesson as a context;**

- **an opportunity for you to understand, through discussion, why certain aspects of your teaching meet with success and others are problematic;**

- **providing you with some reassurance that you are making steady progress towards the induction standards (or, in rare cases, informing you at an early stage that there is much to achieve if you are to meet successfully the induction requirements);**

- **providing evidence which can be used in the formal assessment meetings at the end of each term;**

- **an opportunity for you to establish possible new targets as you review your CEDP at various stages in the induction period;**

- **an opportunity to gain feedback on your teaching from a range of perspectives (induction tutor, head of department, etc).**

Above all, the main purpose is to provide you with feedback and discussion opportunities in relation to your individual path of professional development in the induction period. It is not normally to provide summative judgements about your work.

Who will observe me in the induction period?

One of the main purposes of observation is for you to gain feedback on your teaching from a wide range of different perspectives over the period of the year. This is valuable because, while it may mean that you get different and sometimes conflicting advice and feedback on the same issue, it also means that the observations in the induction period are more valid because more than one perspective is represented. I suggest that there are advantages in at least some of the following providing you with an observation during the course of the induction period.

- **The *induction tutor* is the lead person in supporting your professional development in the induction period and should obviously observe your** teaching, on a number of occasions throughout the year, particularly at the beginning and end of your induction period.

- The *subject co-ordinator* in a primary school, or the *head of department* in a secondary school. Many primary NQTs will have identified particular subject areas at transition point one of the CEDP where strengths and priorities for professional development are defined. This is often the case when a subject has only briefly been addressed in initial teacher training. It makes sense for you to receive at least one observation within these subjects, particularly if it is a focus for your actual targets in the CEDP. In secondary schools, a head of department's observation will be important within your 'main' subject and may also be worthwhile within a subsidiary subject, particularly if you have had little experience of teaching that subject in initial teacher training.

- Your *headteacher* or *deputy headteacher*. Often this will occur at least once in your induction period.

- An LEA inspector/adviser for induction. This will vary from authority to authority, but inspectors/advisers can provide a useful 'outside' perspective in relation to your teaching and can also facilitate ensuing action across a range of schools and situations. LEA inspectors/advisers have multifaceted roles, but during the course of your induction period you may meet one or more of the following:
  - LEA link inspector/adviser (works to a patch of schools)
  - LEA adviser for induction
  - consultants for numeracy, literacy or ICT
  - LEA subject advisers
  - LEA phase advisers (e.g. Early Years).

  The following example provides an indication of the role which an inspector/ adviser may play.

The role of an LEA inspector/adviser in the induction

Dave was an NQT in a three-teacher rural primary school working with Years 3 and 4. The LEA inspector/adviser for induction observed him teaching a science lesson which was related to one of his targets: 'to develop the quality of my teaching of investigative science'. After the observation, it became clear that, while Dave was enjoying much success in his induction period, he needed to consider further the nature of his questioning of children as he set up the investigative science work at the beginning of the lesson. The inspector/adviser was able to liaise with her science colleague and through this conversation Dave visited another school some distance away to observe an 'expert' science co-ordinator teaching a science lesson which had a similar focus in terms of content and style.

What are some of the main approaches to observation?

There are a wide variety of approaches to observing your teaching and children's learning within classrooms. I would argue that it is important for you to know about the various different approaches because different people have different learning styles. For some a heavily structured, bullet-pointed feedback sheet where the observation is broken down into small sections is useful. Others find this unnecessarily fragmented and prefer a holistic approach where there is a narrative which includes analysis of the lesson as it occurred chronologically. In many cases a record of a professional conversation following an observation is included in the critique sheet.

Whatever the approaches to observation, you should be aware of its focus and purpose prior to the observation. This is all the more important because in comparison with your experience in ITT, it is highly likely that observations will be rather less frequent. You will wish to gain as much from each observation as possible. It is therefore worthwhile preparing for the observations and here you may have a role in instigating a short conversation with the observer. You will need to consider at least some of the following factors:

- *How does the observation relate to professional objectives* which you have set in you action plan for the induction year? Here it will be worthwhile to ask for feedback in relation to one or more specific foci.

- *Will the observer have any involvement in the lesson?* It may be that the observer has little or no involvement in the lesson itself, or alternatively s/he may work with a group of pupils during the actual seatwork. A third possibility is to create a collaborative teaching plan when the role of observer and teacher are merged. An example of this relates to primary NQT, Mike, who was having some difficulty with the text level work at the beginning of the literacy hour and in conducting the plenary at the end. In a conversation with his induction tutor prior to the observation, it was decided that the observation would focus only on these two elements, and that the observer would become directly involved in the guided writing work in the middle section of the literacy hour. In this way Mike was receiving feedback which directly and explicitly related to his targets.

- *How will you prepare the children for the observation?* This will clearly depend on your relationship with them and the culture of mentoring within the school. In many schools, observation of teaching by other teachers is a normal part of school life and observation in the induction year will seem an appropriate and ordinary activity.

- *Which lesson will be observed?* Here there are a number of issues which may need addressing before a decision is made. If the purpose of observation is to provide you with feedback about your teaching so that you can develop your practice, there is probably little point in always selecting a lesson where you focus on a specific strength, although to do this on occasion will help you to build on strengths. Anna is a teacher of mathematics in an inner-city comprehensive school and the formal observation focused on a lesson where she was working at a particular area of development. She is well respected and liked by the majority of pupils in her classes, but has some difficulty with her Year 7 groups as she is finding it problematic to find the right level for her pupils. It was therefore agreed that the second observation (in the latter part of the autumn term) would be focused on the pitch of her work with one of the Year 7 maths groups.

- *How do you wish feedback to be organised?* I think that the professional conversation which follows any observation is probably *the* most important part of the whole process. It is therefore worthwhile at the preparation stage considering when the best time is for it to occur. It is important that your observer provides brief informal feedback at the end of the lesson and that s/he knows this is part of the role. It is equally important that time is set aside for a structured analysis of the observation. Ideally, this should be no more than two days after the observation and in many cases this time lapse will provide you with an opportunity to reflect on the lesson, perhaps in order to bring some written response to the meeting.

- *Do you wish to ask for a specific style of written feedback?* **One of the key principles of the induction period arrangements is that induction is done 'with' you as NQT, rather then 'to' you. How can this principle be reflected in the** *style* **of observation? It may be that, in the written comments, questions are asked by the observer and space is left for you to respond as preparation for the tutorial. This then creates a dialogue between you and the observer and encourages you to reflect in a focused way on the observation.**

The preparation phase for any observation is an important part of the process. In ITT, where observation of a lesson may occur every week, it may be unrealistic to undertake observations in all the kinds of ways suggested on every occasion. In the induction period, where observation is much less frequent, the preparation phase needs to be at more depth and should be regarded as an integral part of the whole process.

I now wish to consider various different approaches to observation, to illustrate the range of possibilities from the unstructured to the highly structured. You may wish to use these examples to develop a view about which style you would find to be most helpful.

In Figure II, the first example (primary), there is a fairly unstructured approach which describes the lesson and also includes some analysis within the critique. It is written in the third person and at the end there is a record of the key points which were addressed following the observation.

NEWLY QUALIFIED TEACHER REPORT FORM

Kerry Smith   Date appointed: 01.09.03

Details of class observed, subjects taught, etc

Literacy lesson observed: 2 December 2003
Kerry's responsibilities for the class, organisation, planning, etc. are still as described in the first observation report.

Apart from my observations, Kerry has also been observed by the literacy co-ordinator, music co-ordinator and art co-ordinator and has received feedback from them.

Teaching and class management

This was a well-planned literacy lesson with appropriate and clearly set out teaching objectives. It outlined a clear structure for the lesson and identified differentiated tasks for the groups in the main part of the lesson, following the strategy guidelines. It was clear from the prepared resources and delivery of the shared text, sentence level and word level work in the whole class oral part of the lesson, that Kerry has a high level of pedagogical knowledge and understanding in this area of English.

The lesson began at a brisk pace and it was good to see Kerry review and draw on the children's previous learning. Rachel shared the learning objectives of the lesson and this sharp focus was continued throughout. There was a great deal of consolidation of knowledge skills and understanding with regard to phonemes and graphemes incorporated into the lesson, as well as opportunities to acquire new understanding of word patterns and their sounds and spellings. It was lovely to see that a purposeful working atmosphere was gained and maintained but at the same time the children were interested and motivated enough to share ideas and join in both the questioning aspect of the lesson as well as the interactive session. The introduction of new vocabulary was discussed and encouraged.

The activities for the main part of the lesson were explained carefully and clearly and they were organised in such a way that the children benefited from the maximum support. The guided reading session was overseen by Kerry herself, while the NNEB and I supported two of the other groups. One group was left to work independently. The work was related to the first part of the lesson for three of the groups and reinforced the understanding of phonemes and graphemes as well as introducing some of the children to new vocabulary. The children worked well and were looking to meet targets set by Kerry. The handwriting was of a good standard and on speaking to Kerry after the lesson she was pleased with the work they produced.

The plenary session was a fun activity on the carpet, assessing the children's understanding of rhyming words. All the children managed to contribute to this session and it was good to see the positive ethos developed in the classroom.

Kerry has developed strategies to encourage good behaviour and her consistently high expectations working in conjunction with these strategies produces a pleasant environment in the classroom.

Kerry continues to think about the SEN in the classroom and is constantly questioning the most effective way to enhance the learning of these children.

This was a good lesson in which Kerry engaged the children and sustained their interest and motivation. She has a good working relationship with them.

In our meeting afterwards, the following points were discussed:

- This was a well-planned and delivered literacy lesson.
- Differentiation (CEDP target) continues to be addressed. Today the oral session incorporated high order questioning aimed at different levels of ability. The written work was differentiated accordingly, with individuals having targets to meet, and support was added to help in the differentiation process. Were the highest ability children being challenged enough?
- Behaviour Management (CEDP target) continues to be addressed. Today's evidence showed consistently high expectations, with appropriate measures taken to ensure expectations are met. Positive encouragement helps in this area. Jordan continues to be a challenge but is responding well.
- Displays are bright and attractively presented.
- Personal time management is improving and the reward is the children's personal development.
- Christmas activities are being incorporated into the daily routine and are being organised well.

Well done Kerry. You have continued to develop your expertise in the classroom showing a conscientious approach to everything you do. It is good to see your commitment, and to know that you reflect carefully on your own and the children's progress. Thank you for your help with the ICT. Perhaps next term, now that you have consolidated your work in the classroom, you can become more involved in the training and development of ICT in the school and move onto the update and development of the web site. These are ongoing but important aspects of school life. Thank you.

Figure 11. Semi-open observation with integral feedback section.

In the second example which is in Figure 12 (secondary), the school has used a semi-structured sheet . This observation sheet is fairly broadly based and is organised under the three key areas of the induction standards. Unlike the first example, it does not contain an integral written record of the discussion following the feedback.

NQT INDUCTION
LESSON OBSERVATION RECORD SHEET

Newly qualified teacher: Sian Robbins
Induction tutor: Geoff Smith
Class and subject/topic: Y8 Geography
Date and time: 27/2/03 11.40 a.m.
Focus of observation:

Professional values and practice

You have built purposeful and successful professional relationships within and beyond the Department. You related well to Peter [the geography technician] and included him in your planning. During the next term, I would like to encourage you to be a little more proactive in your own professional development. What are the key things you wish to achieve? How can that be recorded as targets within the CEDP? What kind of support would help you achieve these targets?

Subject knowledge

You dealt with pupils' misconceptions very well, particularly concerning the nature of geographical investigation.

Teaching

The planning for the lesson was good. In particular your objectives were clearly related to the geographical investigation and were specific and focused. Behaviour management was mostly effective and you have a positive rapport with this group of pupils. I wonder whether the conclusion could have developed ideas involved in the validity of the investigation. I felt that the lesson just ended! During the seatwork you circulated well amongst groups of pupils as they planned their investigation. I think your questioning of the children was good and this will have enabled you to gain useful information in relation to the assessment of the lesson. I think an area for development is your marking of pupils' work which has a tendency to be rather brief. Further comments with appropriate questions for response would be helpful.

Figure 12. Semi-structured feedback using the headings of the induction standards.

Figure 13, the third example (primary), is one where a school has used a proforma identical to that supplied by a local ITT institution. This may be particularly useful for the first part of the induction period where the assessment of the period is in relation to the consistent meeting of the QTS standards. The proforma contains a series of prompts which relate to the standards, as well as an integral space for targets to be written in response to the standards.

PROMPTS FOR USE WHEN COMPLETING LESSON OBSERVATION PROFORMAS

This cover sheet details all of the Standards for the Award of Qualified Teacher Status. The text of the Standards has been précised to allow for them all to appear in this form. Some of the Standards are unlikely to be evidenced in the school / setting context but are included here to be comprehensive.
The use of alphabetical labels for each Standard is specific to this proforma and is aimed to assist in report writing, action planning and target setting.

1. PROFESSIONAL VALUES & PRACTICE

a. high expectations of / respect for pupils from all backgrounds (social, cultural, linguistic, religious & ethnic), committed to raising achievement
b. consistent treatment of pupils with respect and consideration, concerned for development
c. demonstrate / promote positive values, attitudes & behaviour
d. communicate sensitively with / recognise role of parents / carers
e. contribute to / share responsibility in corporate life of school / setting
f. understand contribution of support staff / other professionals to teaching and learning
g. evaluate own teaching / learn from others / responsible for own professional development
h. aware of / work within statutory frameworks relating to teachers' responsibilities

2. KNOWLEDGE & UNDERSTANDING

a. secure knowledge / understanding of subjects trained to teach (including, where relevant, six areas of learning of CGFS, NNS, NLS, NC core subject PsoS, & (foundation subjects*))
b. know / understand NC general teaching requirements (including Citiz & PSHE)
c. awareness of key stages / phases before and after one trained for
d. aware of pupils' physical, intellectual, linguistic, social, cultural, emotional development
e. use ICT effectively to teach and support wider professional role
f. understand responsibilities under SEN Code of Practice / know how to seek advice on SEN
g. know a range of behaviour management / purposeful learning environment strategies
h. passed QTS skills tests in numeracy / literacy / ICT

3.1 TEACHING – PLANNING, EXPECTATIONS & TARGETS

a. set challenging / relevant T&L objectives based on: the pupils / evidence of their past and current achievement / expected standards / range and content of work given age range
b. use T&L objectives to plan, sequence and assess for all pupils / take account of and support varying needs of ethnic groups, girls and boys
c. select / prepare / plan for safe and appropriate use of resources accounting for pupil interests / language / cultural backgrounds$^\Phi$
d. work in teaching teams / plan for deployment of additional adults
e. plan for learning in out-of-school contexts$^\Phi$

*with advice from experienced colleague where appropriate
$^\Phi$with help of other staff where appropriate

3.2 TEACHING -- MONITORING & ASSESSMENT

a. monitor and assess pupils to T&L objectives and to inform teaching
b. monitor, assess, give feedback as teaching / encouraging pupil reflection and evaluation
c. assess pupils' progress against NC / ELGs / strategies as appropriate[†]
d. identify / support more able pupils, low achievers and those experiencing behavioural, emotional and social difficulties[†]
e. can identify attainment of pupils' learning Eng as additional language / provide cognitive challenge as well as language support to such pupils[†]
f. record pupils' progress to provide evidence and inform planning
g. use records as a basis for reporting for parents / carers / other professionals and pupils

3.3 TEACHING – TEACHING & CLASS MANAGEMENT

a. establish purposeful working environment based on high expectations and successful relationships with pupils
b. teach expected knowledge, understanding, skills to age range (including, where relevant, six areas of learning of CGFS, NNS, NLS, NC core subject PsoS, & (foundation subjects*))
c. teach structured and motivating lessons with clear learning objectives / interactive approaches / collaborative working / promotion of independent & active learning
d. differentiate teaching to include more able and those with SEN[†]
e. able to support those learning Eng as additional language[†]
f. account for interests / experiences / achievements of boys and girls / those from cultural and ethnic groups
g. organise / manage teaching and learning time effectively
h. organise / manage teaching space and equipment effectively[‡]
i. set high behaviour expectations and manage effectively
j. use ICT effectively in teaching
k. take responsibility for teaching a class over a sustained / substantial period across appropriate age / ability range
l. can provide homework / out-of-class work which consolidates and extends
m. work with specialist teachers / (plan for teaching assistants / other adults[†])
n. recognise / respond to equal opportunities issues, following policies and procedures on stereotyping, bullying and harassment

[†]with guidance / help of an experienced teacher where necessary
[‡]with the help of support staff where necessary

Figure 13. Using a local ITT provider's lesson observation proforma for the first part of the induction period.

LESSON OBSERVATION PROFORMA

Name of Student Teacher .... School ....

Course (Circle as appropriate)	4 Yr BA/BSc(QTS) Y1 Y2 Y3 Y4 PG Full Time Upper Early	3 Yr BA/BSc(QTS) Y1 Y2 Y3 PG Flex-Mod r1 r2 r3 r4	Other

Year group(s)   N   R   1   2   3   4   5   6   Date .... Time .... No. in group ....

Activity ....

Please refer to the Standards Prompts when completing this proforma

General Comment (set context of lesson in terms of theme / topic / subject, desired learning outcomes, NC PoS / NLS / NNS / ELGs covered, lesson structure / format)

Tim – when I came into your classroom today, I observed part of a literacy hour. I feel positive about the fundamentals. At the beginning of the lesson you organised the children very well and your behaviour management was excellent. You were positive and direct with the children. The DLOs were precise and the plan contained an appropriate level of detail. ICT was incorporated into the plans. You used appropriate subject terms in your plan and teaching. In the text level work I am glad that all children had the opportunity to see the text. It is good practice to have the main objective for the lesson visible for the children to see. Could you have made more of this with the class? I also felt that the pace of your whole class work was good and you moved effectively from text to word level work.

Key Observations and Advice

1. There was an issue in relation to your subject knowledge regarding one or two adjectives. Children's misconceptions needed challenging. Were you sure of your ground here?
2. Although the pace was generally good, try not to be distracted by children raising hands, etc.
3. Try to ensure that you actually state your DLO to the children.
4. Your assessment file is variable. History is good. Literacy needs further development. Can you develop a formal, focused assessment in some area of literacy?

Targets for Development and Action Plan (to be completed in tutorial)

1. To ensure that you anticipate possible misconceptions in your teaching of literacy. Consider what these are likely to be when you prepare your lesson plan.
2. To develop an appropriate record of your assessment of children's learning in literacy. Liaise with the Literacy Co-ordinator to ensure that what you decide to do is in line with whole school policy.

White copy: retained by student   Yellow copy: to be sent to student's base campus School Partnership Office   Pink copy: retained by school

Signed .... (tutor)   Signed .... (student)

Figure 13 (continued). Using a local ITT provider's lesson observation proforma for the first part of the induction period.

This kind of approach is taken further in a final example, Figure 14, where comments are made in relation to each area of the induction standards. The school used this proforma during terms two and three of the induction period. This is a primary example and as will be seen from the report, the fact that the report has been grounded in the induction standards means that it has a much wider brief than the actual lesson which has been observed.

What are the characteristics of effective discussion following an observation?

I mentioned earlier in this section that the discussion which follows an observation is probably the most important strategy to ensure your professional development. There is much to be gained from a specific, sharply focused conversation based on a shared experience. However, it is easy for the potential of these discussions not to be realised and it is worthwhile taking a few simple steps as you undertake your role in managing how the post-observation session is set up. Some of these points are also mentioned in Chapter 4 where there is a section on the formal assessment meeting. Others apply particularly to these kinds of professional discussions.

- **Ensure that the discussion is a *dialogue*, not you being 'fed back to'. You may need to intervene with your perspective on the lesson or to ask for justification or elaboration of a point. I feel that it is best if the style of the discussion is established before or at the start of the meeting, so that you and your induction tutor are clear about its nature.**

- **If your post-observation session is a couple of days after the actual event, then it will be worth you bringing a *written reflection* of the observation to the meeting, identifying strengths and areas for development. I think some of the best discussions occur where both observed and observer have a very clear idea of the key points in relation to the lesson.**

- **Agree a *start and end point* for the discussion. There is no need for the discussion to be long and laborious, particularly if both parties bring a considered reflection to the meeting.**

- **You need to be very clear about *actions* which will be taken by yourself and others as a result of the discussion. These may be related to the CEDP targets and will certainly need to be specific, but manageable. However, the overriding point is that there is no value in the meeting if there if no ensuing action. The potential of the discussion will certainly not be met in this circumstance.**

- **Although I believe observation of teaching cannot ever be totally 'objective', it is also true that wherever possible the discussion needs to be based on *evidence* which is clear to both parties.**

- **It is useful to have a *brief written record* of the outcome of the discussion. In some cases, this will be an integral part of the observation proforma (see Figures 11 and 13). In other cases, it will be written according to a series of simple headings such as: main focus of the discussion; targets; action; plan for review. You may wish to consider using the example proforma in Figure 15 to record your discussions.**

NQT Induction: Lesson Observation Record Sheet

Newly Qualified Teacher	*Irene Roberts*
Induction Tutor	*Sally Green*
Class and subject/topic	*Reception: numeracy*
Date and time	*15/05/00 10.45am*
Focus of Observation	*numeracy*

Standards	Notes
1 Professional Values and Practice	You have clearly set objectives at transition point two which you are meeting. You are able to talk about how you are meeting these. Would you consider attending the LEA Early Years Numeracy course next term? This may help you build on the excellent work that I have seen today.
	Your work with Elaine *[the nursery nurse]* is excellent and during the numeracy lesson she had a very clear role. You discuss your planning with her and I know that she feels very much included in the life of your classroom
2 Knowledge and Understanding	Your ability to address children's misconceptions was very much in evidence. You used a wide range of strategies, including ICT, practical work and role play.
3 Teaching 3.1 Planning, expectations and targets	Can we discuss how you've used baseline assessment to inform targets for pupils in the review meeting?
	Differentiation was in evidence, particularly in regard to children who are not yet able to recognise numbers to 10.
	Could you have extended the activity further for Tom and Tina who are clearly able to recognise numbers to 20?
3.2 Monitoring and Assessment	I feel that your numeracy assessments for lower achieving children are good and generally accurate, but there is a need to use assessments for more able children more effectively.
	There is much anecdotal evidence that you have liaised effectively with parents, for example regarding the whole school reading record. In our next review meeting I would suggest that we consider your approach to formal report writing.
3.3 Teaching and Class Management	The management of pupil behaviour was excellent. You had clear expectations and the children understood these. Your organisation of children enabled you to pre-empt any inappropriate behaviour.
	I know that since my last observation, you have been involved in Jack's IEP and it is good to see evidence of you relating this to your planning and teaching of the numeracy hour.
	There is much evidence in the classroom that you have put into practice the assertive discipline policy that exists within school.

Figure 14. Observation in relation to the induction standards.

RECORD OF POST-OBSERVATION DISCUSSION

Name of NQT:

Name of Induction Tutor:

Date:

Main foci of discussion:

*

*

*

*

*

*

Main points of action	How do these relate to objectives at transition point 2 of the CEDP?
*	
*	
*	
*	
*	
*	

Figure 15. Record of post-observation discussion.

- **It is important that action which follows from the discussion relates to the objectives that have already been agreed and recorded in the CEDP. If there is no obvious link, there is a danger that the management of your professional development becomes fragmented with too many disparate objectives and actions. The guiding principle is that the discussion meeting and the observation itself should have some kind of link with the objectives which you have established for the induction period.**

Section Three

Beyond observation – approaches to supporting your development as an NQT

The previous section has considered the roles of observation of you teaching and feedback from observations in the development of your practice as a teacher. This part of the chapter considers a number of other approaches to support your professional development. During the course of the induction year it would not be the case that you necessarily experience all of these, but in presenting them here I hope that you are aware of a number of different possibilities as you devise action to meet the targets which you have set.

Setting up a programme of professional development

One of the things which has been emphasised throughout this book is the issue of an individually determined path of professional development in the induction period. Your CEDP established individual objectives and actions, and, as a result of these, each NQT should have an element of individuality in their experience of the year. Just as many of the objectives are individual, so too will be the professional development plans.

It is in this sense that your induction tutor has a key role in ensuring that arrangements for appropriate professional development activities are specific to you as an NQT. One of the TTA support national booklets states that the induction tutor has a role in:

> organising and implementing, in consultation with the NQT, a tailored programme of monitoring, support and assessment which takes forward in a flexible way the action plan set out in the NQT's Career Entry Profile and which takes account of the needs and strengths identified in the Profile, the Induction Standards and the specific context of the school.
>
> (TTA 1999a, p. 12)

It is important that there is recognition of the 10% reduction in teaching load. The whole point of this is that you have some additional time and space to undertake activities directly related to your professional development. It may be that you have additional free periods (secondary) or a whole morning (primary) every week, or it is possible that the time is blocked so that you have a more substantial period to engage in professional development activities, perhaps lasting three days or so at various times of the year. While the detail of how your professional development plan will vary in different kinds of schools, the critical elements are that:

(a) You have a 10% reduction in teaching load (that is, you teach 90% of the normal average teaching duties for your school).

(b) The time is not additional time for routine tasks, such as planning, evaluation or record-keeping. It is specifically for your professional development.

I want to develop an actual example of how this process may work so that you can see what may be possible. The example is from an NQT, Rebecca, working with a Year 2 class. It is a real example, but I have modified it to show the kinds of support which may be possible. It relates to the autumn term of the NQT's induction period. In the first instance, an action plan was developed following discussions at transition point two. This was completed with the induction tutor. You can see this as Figure 16 and you will notice that there are three key areas which Rebecca is addressing. These relate to:

- **behaviour management skills;**
- **provision for special educational needs;**
- **developing subject co-ordination skills in ICT.**

As a result of objectives in these three areas being established, actions were identified which led to the following professional development activities in the autumn term:

In relation to the behaviour management skills focus

- **A focused observation of a parallel Year 1 class teacher managing circle time and building children's self-esteem (end of September).**
- **A structured discussion following this observation (end of September).**
- **Collaborative teaching with an experienced teacher to embed observed strategies into Rebecca's own practice (mid-October).**

In relation to the SEN focus

- **Hold a structured conversation with the school's SENCO to acquire copies of the IEPs and to understand the school's policy and practice in this area (mid-September).**
- **Attendance at a one-day course relating to integration of children with Special Educational Needs into the mainstream classroom (mid-November).**
- **Observation of the SENCO working with a child with moderate learning difficulties in literacy (mid-November).**
- **Advisory conversation with SENCO about how to modify literacy tasks to suit the needs of statemented children (mid-October).**
- **Review of progress made over the term with the SENCO (early December).**

In relation to the subject co-ordination focus

- **Visit another school to talk with an ICT co-ordinator and consider how the policy in that school has been developed and put into practice (early November).**

Induction Year: Transition Point Two

OBJECTIVES AND ACTION PLANS FOR THE INDUCTION PERIOD

OBJECTIVES	ACTIONS TO BE TAKEN AND BY WHOM	SUCCESS CRITERIA	RESOURCES	TARGET DATE FOR ACHIEVEMENT	REVIEW DATE
Develop appropriate strategies for dealing with pupils' behaviour - extend routines to suit my class of children. Develop new management methods in addition to this.	Establish rules for the class - continue to reinforce and adapt if necessary. Observe other classroom practice to gain a wider insight into other options.	Level and quantity of work increased. Less time spent on routines and administration.	Classroom rules - display? Observation time to go to other classes.	By end of Autumn half term. ①	
Extend knowledge of SEN in class 5 - and develop appropriate differentiated tasks for specific children / groups.	Continue to assess, monitor and review work set. Begin to adapt tasks further to suit children's specific needs. Speak to SENCO to acquire IEPs and other information.	Lower ability groups will progress at their own level. SEN children will increase their independence when working and become more confident to complete tasks unaided.	Speak to SENCO - acquire SEN records to assess starting point and project achievements.	Within Autumn term. ①	
Develop subject co-ordination skills and work within ICT. Undertake activities within schools alongside ICT co-ordinator to gain further skills / knowledge.	Keep up to date with whole school ICT development - discussion with HC. Develop ICT opportunities within class 5 - use this knowledge to discuss with other NQT teachers.	ICT will be used frequently and purposefully within whole curriculum. Attendance of meetings relating to ICT in school.	Speak to ICT co-ordinator. ICT plans - review and develop.		

Signature on behalf of school	Date	Signature of NQT	Date

Figure 16. Rebecca's action plan (transition point two).

NQT Programme: The Role of the Co-ordinator

Course No. CRS/CPD/   Beacon School Funded

12.45   Coffee

Aims of the session:

- To provide a forum for the critical examination and discussion of the role of the primary curriculum co-ordinator.
- To allow NQT co-ordinators the opportunity to examine good practice and to relate this to their own school setting.
- By the end of the session you will know more about the expectations schools place on co-ordinators and be able to deal more confidently with your role in school.

13.00   Introduction

Welcome and outline of afternoon given by Deputy Head.

What is the role of the co-ordinator?
Where do you start?
Looking at various aspects of the co-ordinator's role and critically analysing them.

Moving forward – Matches and mismatches with Curriculum 2000.

Group work: How can you monitor the implementation of the schemes of work throughout the school?

Feedback and discussion.
Examples of our practice and how it is delivered.

How do you as co-ordinator respond to the strengths and weaknesses observed during the monitoring process?
Group work: Scenarios.

Feedback and discussion.

Devise realistic action plan for own curriculum area for the rest of this year.

15.00   Questions and evaluation

Figure 17. An example of a professional development activity implemented as part of the professional development programme for Rebecca.

- **Shadow the ICT co-ordinator in the planning and delivery of a staff meeting focused on the development of ICT within the school (mid-November).**
- **Lead a follow-through INSET session with a small group of KS1 colleagues (late November). Prepare this in consultation with the ICT co-ordinator.**

Rebecca James, Year 2   Induction tutor: Bob White
Programme of Professional Development Activities
Autumn 2000

4 September 2.30pm	Meet with Bob White to provide information on key school routines (part of INSET day in school).
11 September 3.45pm	Meet with induction tutor to set key objectives and actions for term 1.
18 September 1.00-3.30pm	Focused observation of class 4 on how Rebecca manages circle time with the children, and including a structured discussion about this.
22 September 9. 15-10. 15am	Observation of Rebecca teaching a literacy hour (Bob White).
8 October 1.00-3.40pm	First professional review meeting with Bob White, focusing on key objectives relating to the development of behaviour management skills.

Figure 18. Excerpt from Rebecca's professional development programme.

- **Observe the teaching of ICT in the computer room (early December).**

- **Attend session set up for NQTs in the local area relating to the role of the co-ordinator (mid-October). The programme for this is in Figure 17.**

Once objectives have been set and action plans written, it will be possible not only to devise the professional development programme for the term, but also to integrate this with key activities in the induction period such as the professional review meetings (see Section Four of this chapter), observations of teaching and formal assessment meetings (see Chapter 4). In Rebecca's case an excerpt from her programme may look something like Figure 18.

What are the kinds of professional development activities which I could experience as an NQT?

Here I consider four main kinds of professional development activities. These are not intended to be exhaustive, but do give an indication of the main kinds of such activity which are of particular benefit and interest. They are:

- **observation of other teachers;**
- **collaborative planning and teaching;**
- **visits to other schools;**
- **informal guidance.**

OBSERVATION OF OTHER TEACHERS
This is perhaps the most frequently adopted activity and I believe that it has enormous potential to lead to effective professional development if it is set up properly. I think that the key thing is for the focus of observation to be clearly defined and related to your professional objectives and actions. Two examples will be used to illustrate possible approaches.

NQT Programme: Numeracy

Course No. CRS/CPD/18 – Beacon School Funded

08.30	Arrival Outline of morning given by Deputy Head
08.40	Meet teacher whose lesson and class you will observe. Quick résumé of lesson and objectives: weekly plan with today's lesson highlighted will be given to you.
09.00-10.00	Numeracy lesson observation. Look at management, groupings, seating, organisation, etc.

Observation of **oral and mental session.**

Main activity: Observe how the children are grouped, what each group is asked to do, and how the teacher organises and manages the group work. Observe how she monitors the children's work, facilitates learning and helps the children to progress. Feel free to walk around and observe the children and use this time to stand back and reflect how a numeracy lesson is planned and managed after one term of being fully involved and immersed in the process yourself.

Plenary: Observe the strategies used for this part of the lesson. How does it fit in with the rest of the lesson?

Figure 19. Programme for NQTs' observation of the teaching of numeracy.

Carl is a secondary NQT working within the English department of a comprehensive school in a market town in the north of England. During the course of the first term of the induction period, it became apparent that Carl was having some difficulty in pitching the level of his work for his Year 9 group, in particular regarding the way in which he was encouraging pupils to produce various kinds of written responses to set texts. This issue was reflected in one of his CEDP objectives for the spring term, namely 'to be able to facilitate a high quality of pupil written response to set texts (Year 9)'. It was agreed that for a period of two weeks, Carl would shadow his colleague Wendy's work with a parallel Year 9 group. This involved collaborative planning, focused observation of Wendy's teaching, discussion with Wendy and implementation of the qualities which Carl wished to emulate. The strategy was effective, not least because the timetable of the school meant that the two different groups of pupils were taught at different times of the week. This meant that Carl was able to observe on Monday and then put the results of these observations into practice on Thursday. This led to a significant increase in the quality of Carl's teaching, and, in particular, he had a much clearer idea about the quality of written response that was expected from a Year 9 pupil in his particular school. For him, the mixture of observation, discussion and feedback had been very important in developing his practice. He felt supported and challenged, and the fact that the observation was focused and specific was particularly pertinent.

A second example is taken from a primary school situated in a large town, again in the north of England. This school enjoys Beacon school status and as such provides a programme of support for NQTs from the LEA. Part of this programme involves a full morning on numeracy, including a focused observation with key questions in relation to the different aspects of the numeracy hour. The programme for the morning can be seen in Figure 19 and I have included it here because it provides a very good example of the potential of observation. In this sense:

- **The context of the observation is established. There is an opportunity to view the planning, including the particular lesson in a short discussion with the class teacher.**
- **The focus of the observation is specified and a range of questions are posed to which the NQTs are encouraged to make a response.**
- **There is a short opportunity to discuss points seen in the observation with the class teacher.**
- **There is an opportunity for a wider discussion drawing a number of key points from the observation. This element is particularly worthwhile because it can be used to identify specific points for action in the NQT's own targets.**

COLLABORATIVE PLANNING AND TEACHING

The value of collaborative planning and teaching has already been mentioned in section two of this chapter, but there is space here to consider it in more detail. Collaborative planning and teaching are good professional development activities, particularly if the nature of the issue to be addressed is very specific. Examples may include:

- **an NQT teaching Early Years children who wishes to develop his ability to engage children in appropriate discussion during semi-structured play activities;**
- **a secondary history NQT who has difficulties with working with individual children while monitoring the whole class during seatwork;**
- **a primary NQT whose literacy hour plenaries have a tendency to focus on what the children have done rather than what they have learned;**
- **a secondary MFL NQT who has difficulty in managing the behaviour of a small group of girls in her Year 8 group;**
- **a secondary maths NQT who wishes his introduction to a Year 7 group to include more practical and interactive demonstrations.**

Collaborative planning and teaching involves the NQT and the experienced teacher, who may or may not be an induction tutor, planning in detail a lesson which they will jointly lead. The main point of this is that the NQT and the experienced teacher are both very clear about their roles and that the experienced teacher's role includes teaching that part of the lesson which relates to the focus for the NQT. The NQT can observe at this point and teach remaining parts of the lesson while the experienced teacher works alongside her in collaboration. Take the final example above relating to a secondary maths NQT who is experiencing difficulties with introductions. During the collaboratively taught lesson the experienced teacher would teach the initial part of the lesson, hence modelling for the NQT an area of teaching which he found difficult, namely practical demonstrations during introductions for a Year 7 class. The NQT would observe this teaching and then during the part of the lesson where pupils are working

LESSON PLAN FOR COLLABORATIVE TEACHING

Age group of children

Number of children

Date of lesson

Duration of lesson

Key focus for NQT

Key Lesson Objectives	Links to NC POS

Key Vocabulary to be used in the lesson

Lesson content and roles

Times	What will pupils be doing? (including notes on differentiation)	Role of NQT	Role of Experienced Teacher

Figure 20. Planning for collaborative teaching.

independently on tasks would collaboratively teach with the experienced teacher. The lesson would end with the NQT taking the plenary while the experienced teacher observed, prior to a review of the whole process.

In order to get the most out of collaborative planning and teaching, I believe it is best to use a detailed planning format which specifically plans for different roles within the lesson. It may also be important to have an established culture whereby collaboration and joint working is not seen as unusual by class participants. A suggested proforma for collaborative planning is provided in Figure 20.

VISITS TO OTHER SCHOOLS

As with collaborative planning and teaching, visits to other schools are a useful part of your induction programme if they have a sharp focus and purpose. If their purpose is not apparent or a focus not defined, then their benefit will be compromised. The following are examples of specific purposes:

- **As an** *NQT in a small rural primary school,* **you may have a limited range of role models to model good practice. One strategy to address this is for NQTs in two or more small schools to arrange observations of teaching in each other's schools and then meet for discussion and feedback.**
- **As a** *secondary NQT,* **a key issue for you may be transition between Key Stages 2 and 3. You may wish to visit a primary school to develop your understanding of what occurs in Key Stage 2 prior to transfer.**
- **As a** *music secondary NQT,* **you may be working in very small department, and while you have general support from colleagues in other departments you would benefit from visiting another school to develop your understanding of different approaches to teaching music.**
- **You are having some difficulty in managing the** *behaviour of your Year 6* **class in a positive way. Arrangements are made for you to visit another school where circle time is used effectively as a strategy for managing behaviour in a positive proactive manner.**

INFORMAL GUIDANCE

One of the features of the new induction arrangements is that there is a degree of formality, in terms of both your assessment and the approaches to support and monitoring which are undertaken by the school. I think it may be important for you to have a professional friend who can provide day-to-day guidance on issues of immediate concern. These may be as diverse as the provision of basic information when you start in school and advice on dealing with a difficult parent, but the general point is that there will be occurrences to which you need to respond as quickly as possible.

In one large primary school, the role of professional friend was built into the roles and responsibilities of people associated with the induction year. Members of the senior management team were responsible for the formal assessment of all the NQTs in school, induction tutors organised an induction programme based on NQTs' objectives and action plans, and each NQT also had a nominated 'professional friend' who could provide advice and information in relation to specific classroom events as they arose. In this school, the 'assessor role' was formally separated from the 'educator role' and the 'professional friend/counsellor' role. NQTs felt that the system worked well, as there was clarity of role. For the whole school, there were also pay-offs as the distribution of roles meant that most experienced staff had some kind of formal role with the NQTs. This meant that there was a perception that the whole school recognised its responsibilities to the mentoring process generally and to NQTs specifically.

In addition to the professional friend idea, you should also receive guidance from colleagues in regard to your stated individualised needs in relation to the induction standards. Examples may include working alongside the SENCO, receiving input from subject leaders, considering the school's approach to equal opportunities or working with a health and safety co-ordinator.

I have chosen to emphasise these four kinds of professional development activities because these relate to you as an individual NQT. The roles of focused observation and collaborative teaching are, I believe, particularly pertinent in ensuring that professional development is systematic and effective. Additionally, there will be opportunities for you to become involved in more general professional development opportunities such as courses for NQTs laid on by your LEA, local conferences and events organised by subject and professional associations and opportunities for you to work towards a further qualification. In regard to the latter, one higher education institution provides an opportunity for NQTs to log their activities in a structured professional development file which can lead to the award of an advanced qualification. An example of an event organised by a professional association is a numeracy conference set up by a local branch of the Association for the Study of Primary Education (ASPE). The one-day event attracted a large number of primary teachers including NQTs and combined keynote inputs from local and national speakers and an opportunity for dialogue and debate about the numeracy strategy.

These kinds of activities are, of course, worthwhile and important, but they are not the same as the carefully instigated programmes of individual professional development activities tailored to your needs as an NQT. The essence of the induction period is the idea of individual, systematic professional development. I believe that if this is established following detailed discussion with induction tutors it will ensure that your experience as an NQT is supportive, challenging and rewarding.

Professional review meetings

During the course of your induction period, it is normally the case that you should experience at least six professional review meetings, one towards the end of each half-term. Professional review meetings are an opportunity for you to meet with your induction tutor to review your overall progress towards objectives which you have agreed in the action planning process for the induction period and which you have recorded using an appropriate proforma. These meetings are different from feedback that you may receive after a lesson observation, and they are also different from the formal assessment meetings which occur three times in the induction period. These are considered in some detail in Chapter 4, and are concerned with the extent to which you have met the requirements of the induction period.

What does a professional review meeting involve?

The review meeting is a formal meeting normally between yourself and your induction tutor, and it is important that an agenda is set so you are clear about the meeting's scope and purpose. The following example provides an indication of the nature of a typical review meeting.

Section Four

Phil is a secondary NQT working in a large geography department in a suburban comprehensive school. At the beginning of the induction period, he established three targets to be achieved in the autumn and spring terms. These were:

1. 'To develop an enhanced understanding of assessment criteria at Key Stage 4 of both coursework and examination practice.'
2. 'To ensure that IEPs are understood and that I take more account of these in meeting the needs of individual children.'
3. 'To develop my ability to assess pupils' levels against attainment targets particularly at Key Stage 2.'

A range of actions had been put in place to ensure that Phil had every opportunity to record his targets and these were recorded using an appropriate proforma. The agenda for the professional review meeting towards the end of the spring term focused on the first two objectives because the target date for achievement was at the end of that term. The third objective had been achieved in the autumn term. Figure 21 represents the agenda for this professional review meeting.

An alternative approach to agenda setting is rather less formal and uses key questions to establish the foci for the meeting. In Phil's case the agenda may have looked something like Figure 22.

Professional Review Meeting
Thursday 20 March, 2.00 – 3.00pm

Phil Hunter (NQT), Caroline Young (Induction Tutor)

AGENDA

1. Purpose of meeting.

2. Consideration of objective 1: 'To develop an enhanced understanding of assessment criteria at Key Stage 4 of both coursework and examination practice.' Phil to table his self-assessment document.

3. Consideration of objective 2: 'To ensure that IEPs are understood and that I take more account of these in meeting the needs of individual children.' Caroline to report on her meeting with Paul (the SENCO) which focused on Phil's meeting of this target.

4. Review of the appropriateness of professional activities in relation to the achievements of key objectives.

5. Establishing objectives and actions for the summer term.

6. General review of Phil's achievement in relation to the requirements of the induction period.

7. Date of next review meeting.

Figure 21. Agenda for Phil's professional review meeting.

Professional Review Meeting
Thursday 20 March, 2.00 – 3.00pm

Phil Hunter (NQT), Caroline Young (Induction Tutor)

AGENDA

1. What are the main purposes of the meeting?

2. Has objective 1 been met? Consider Phil's self-assessment of this.

3. Has objective 2 been met? Consider Caroline's discussion with Paul (the school's SENCO).

4. Have professional activities been helpful in meeting key objectives?

5. What further objectives and actions may be appropriate for the summer term?

6. Are there any issues to raise in regard to Phil meeting the requirements of the induction period?

7. Date of next review meeting.

Figure 22. Less formal agenda for a professional review meeting.

You will notice that the first item on the agenda relates to a statement about the purposes of the meeting. I think that, generally, there are at least six purposes of review meetings:

• **to consider a range of evidence in regard to the meeting of specific objectives;**

• **to ensure that the appropriateness of professional development activities is reviewed;**

• **to set new objectives for the next half-term;**

• **to agree how these will be reviewed and monitored;**

• **to ensure that professional development activities to support the process are appropriate and worthwhile;**

• **to consider whether there are any emerging issues in relation to meeting the requirements of the induction period.**

It will be helpful if you bring to the meeting sample evidence that you have met the agreed objectives. This is important if you are to be part of the review process. It is in line with the principle that induction should be done with you and not to you. In Phil's case, sample evidence in relation to objective 1 included:

- examples of annotated marking, showing how he had marked a range of coursework in relation to key assessment criteria;

- a brief account of a moderation meeting with another member of the geography department;

- a lesson plan which showed how he had made the assessment criteria explicit to pupils in advance of the coursework;

- notes from a standardisation meeting set up by the examination board.

The evidence was fairly minimal in terms of quantity. Phil and Caroline had agreed prior to the meeting that their discussion would be enhanced by a focused consideration of specific items of evidence, rather than a brief overview of a large amount of material. This, in turn, made the whole process more manageable.

I have already established that there is a difference between the nature of the professional review meeting and the formal assessment meeting. It is not the role of the professional review meeting to engage in the systematic assessment of either the induction standards or the consistent meeting of the QTS standards. However, it is useful if your overall progress towards the induction year requirements is a standing item on the agenda for professional review meetings. This will provide an opportunity for your induction tutor to raise any issues of concern, or note any areas where you have met with success. It also gives you the opportunity to be reassured that you are making sound progress, or know if there are any aspects of your practice which need addressing prior to the formal assessment meeting.

How can I prepare for the professional review meeting?

The professional review meeting is an ideal opportunity for you to take stock of your achievements in the induction period in relation to the objectives in your action plan and the progress towards the requirements of the induction year. You may wish to undertake some specific self-review prior to the professional review meeting itself and there are a number of strategies which you could use. It is not suggested that you necessarily use all of these. This would probably be unmanageable, but you may wish to adopt one or more as you prepare for the review meeting.

- *Recording classroom snapshots.* This is where for a short period of time you record classroom events relating to one or more of your professional objectives so that you have an account of some detailed examples about which you can talk with your induction tutor. You may wish to refer to Chapter 4, Section Five which provides further details.

- *Evaluation against the induction standards.* Here you may wish to use the target wheel which you can also find in Chapter 4, Section Five. This enables you to consider how you are making progress in relation to all the induction standards, and gives you an 'at a glance' overview.

- *Complete a self-audit of your action plan.* This involves you reflecting at depth on its elements and provides you with an opportunity to consider the appropriateness of the action plan. A suggested proforma for this can be seen in Figure 23.

- *Undertake an evaluation of a single lesson at depth.* This may be particularly useful if you are unsure about the nature of future objectives for your action plan. Specific evaluation may help you to identify areas for you to focus on. It needs to be emphasised that evaluation of a series of lessons is unmanageable and probably inappropriate and this kind of evaluation would be different from the sort you undertook in ITT. You may wish to use the proforma in Figure 24.

- *Complete a log of your professional development programme.* The purpose of this is so that you are clear about which activities have been particularly useful and which less so. It may be that you wish to define 'usefulness' in terms of its impact on how you have been able to achieve your objectives. A suggested proforma for this is provided in Figure 25.

How should the professional review meeting be conducted?

In Chapter 4 there is a section on the formal assessment meetings in the induction year and how these should be managed. It is true that some of the issues there also apply to professional review meetings and I do not wish to repeat the details here; suffice to say that you will wish to consider aspects such as the appropriateness of the venue, the agenda-setting prior to the meeting and the extent to which evidence should be cited. The professional review meetings are, however, different from the assessment meetings and there are a number of specific things which you may wish to bear in mind as you consider the meeting. It may well be appropriate for you to share these with your induction tutor and if you adopt these you will have more control over the review process.

- **The main purpose of the meeting is for there to be some constructive evaluation of your practice and your meeting of objectives. It is not a summative assessment of your work and you will wish the meeting to be carried out in an atmosphere which is conducive to professional dialogue.**

- *Your* **evaluation of how you have met the objectives in your action plan is probably the most important element of the meeting.**

- **In addition to sharing your thoughts you may wish to ask your induction tutor to evaluate the nature of the support which has been given to you. Does** *s/he* **feel it is appropriate?**

- **You need to ask whether actions planned at previous professional review meetings have occurred, not just in relation to your commitments, but particularly actions which others committed themselves to as a result of the process.**

REVIEWING PROGRESS TOWARDS THE ACTION PLAN

Key Question		Comment
Have I achieved the objectives which were set?	OBJ 1	
	OBJ 2	
	OBJ 3	
What evidence do I wish to cite that these objectives have been met?	OBJ 1	
	OBJ 2	
	OBJ 3	
In retrospect to what extent were my objectives focused and precise in nature?		
In what ways did I receive appropriate support in helping me to meet these objectives?		
Were there any further professional development activities which would have been helpful?		
To what extent was the action planned appropriate and sufficient to meet the objectives?		
Were the success criteria tightly linked with the objectives themselves?		
Are there any key points for action which will help ensure that my next action plan becomes more effective?		1. 2.
Which areas will be most appropriate for my next set of objectives and my next action plan?		

Figure 23. Reviewing progress towards the action plan.

EVALUATION PROFORMA

CHECKLIST

ANALYSIS

PLANNING	Y	N	N/A
Were my objectives appropriate?			
Did they relate to the lesson content?			
Did I plan for assessment?			
Did I have a time plan for the lesson?			
Did I plan for differentiation?			
INTRODUCTION			
Did I gain children's attention and hold this through the lesson?			
Was my introduction well paced and structured?			
Did I use appropriate questions?			
Did the children understand what they had to do in their seatwork?			
Was the introduction the right length?			
MAIN BODY OF THE LESSON			
Was children's behaviour appropriate?			
Did the lesson meet the needs of all children?			
Did I find time to work with individuals and groups?			
Did I intervene properly in children's learning?			
Were my expectations high enough?			
Was I happy with the noise level?			
CONCLUSION			
Was there an appropriate plenary?			
Did this focus on what the children had learnt? (as opposed to what they had done?)			
Did I set appropriate homework?			
Did I assess the lesson appropriately using the main objectives?			
OTHER KEY QUESTIONS YOU WISH TO ASK YOURSELF			
•			
•			
•			

From the checklist take one issue for further consideration. This would normally be one where you have answered 'no':

ISSUE _____

Identify possible *causes* of why this was not achieved.

-
-
-

What do I wish to achieve in moving my practice forward in this area?

-

How could I achieve this?

-

Figure 24. Evaluation format (for reflecting on a single lesson).

RECORD OF PROFESSIONAL DEVELOPMENT ACTIVITIES

Date	What kinds of activity? (e.g. course, observations of another teacher, observation of my teaching, etc.)	Locations (as appropriate)	To which objective did the activity relate?	How has the activity impacted on my practice?

Figure 25. Professional development activities.

- You need to have a record of the professional review meeting (see **Figure 26**) and I would suggest it is appropriate for you to write this record either during the course of the meeting or immediately afterwards. This will mark the meeting as being fundamentally different from the assessment meeting where the report is written about you. It may be, however, that your induction tutor undertakes to complete the record, in which case you should have an input to this and, of course, receive a copy.

- It is also important that your professional action plan is updated in the light of the review meeting. This may mean rewriting the action plan, or simply adding to or annotating an earlier plan.

RECORD OF A PROFESSIONAL REVIEW MEETING

Date

Present   (NQT)   (Induction Tutor)

Review of Objective 1 (from action plan)
Has this been achieved?
What evidence is there?
In what ways have planned actions helped me to achieve this objective?
Possible next steps.
Review of Objective 2 (from action plan)
Has this been achieved?
What evidence is there?
In what ways have planned actions helped me to achieve this objective?
Possible next steps.

Possible New Objectives	Possible actions

Figure 26. Record of professional review meeting.

In this chapter you will find material to support you in the following areas:

- **the main requirements in relation to the assessment of the induction period;**
- **the criteria for assessing the induction period;**
- **the formal assessment meetings;**
- **the amount of evidence you need to collect;**
- **what to do if you are at risk of not passing the induction period.**

Introduction and chapter overview

The main purpose of this chapter is to provide you with practical information and support relating to the assessment of your induction period. There are a number of key sections:

- *Section One: the assessment of your induction period – some key questions answered.* **This addresses a wide range of common concerns about the assessment process. Is it like final teaching practice all over again? Who is involved in the process? What happens if I'm at risk of not meeting the induction period requirements? What kinds of evidence are needed?**

- *Section Two: an overview of the formal assessment requirements in the induction period – what happens at various points in the year?* **This section takes you through the assessment process term by term and provides information about the key events.**

- *Section Three: the assessment of the standards – what to look for.* **Here there is a focus on the kinds of things that induction tutors will be looking for as they assess the induction year. It also provides you with a strategy to assess your own practice and be aware of your achievements and areas for development.**

- *Section Four: setting up the formal assessment meetings.* **This considers in more detail approaches to the assessment meeting in terms 1, 2 and 3 and, in particular, notes the importance of clear agenda-setting and defined outcomes.**

- *Section Five: use of evidence in the assessment meetings.* **Practical examples are used to illustrate different forms of evidence and how these can be used productively in the actual meeting.**

- *Section Six: what happens if I am at risk of failing the induction year?* **This final section offers clear advice for the very small minority of NQTs who may be in this position.**

Section One

The assessment of your induction period: some key questions answered

This section of the chapter should help you get your mind straight about the assessment of your induction period. You will see that it is *not* the same as having your final placement assessed all over again and that in many ways and in most cases, it is less onerous and detailed when compared with previous assessments of your teaching prior to qualification. Through reading this section, I hope you will be very clear about the nature of the assessment which is built into the national induction period arrangements. I have organised what follows using a question and answer format.

• **What are the criteria for satisfactory completion of the induction period?**

During your initial training you will have already shown that you have met the standards for the award of QTS. The induction period assessment builds on this in two key ways:

(a) You will be assessed on whether you are able *consistently* to meet the QTS standards over the period of induction and meet these with increasing professional competence. While you will have already spent substantial periods of time in the classroom on teaching practices and other forms of school-based training, you will not have had the opportunity to sustain this for a longer period of time equivalent to the induction period. Additionally, it may well be the case that some aspects of the QTS standards have been securely achieved but with support from experienced teachers. In the induction period you are required to develop your practice further, so that you are able to act independently in all aspects of the QTS standards. The extent to which you are consistently meeting the QTS standards will be the focus of the first term of your induction period in most cases.

(b) In addition to the consistent meeting of the QTS standards you will also need to demonstrate that you have met the induction standards which have been laid down by the DfES (see Figure 27). As you can see, they are much less extensive than the QTS standards and are designed to show progression in the professional expectations of new teachers. In most cases, you will be assessed against the induction standards at the end of the second term of the induction period.

• **Is the assessment of the induction period the same as being reassessed on final teaching practice?**

The straight answer is no! You will already have had a detailed assessment of the standards for the award of QTS. The induction period assessment does *not* involve a detailed reassessment of these standards. It is a much more broadly based judgement about your work which is recorded briefly on a report proforma. The only exception to this would be in the very small minority of cases where the school had a concern about whether you are meeting the induction standards and here the school would need to make more detailed assessments about your work.

The Induction Standards

In order to complete the induction period satisfactorily, a newly qualified teacher must demonstrate all of the following.

Professional Values and Practice

a) seek and use opportunities to work collaboratively with colleagues to raise standards by sharing effective practice in the school.

Knowledge and Understanding

They continue to meet the requirements of the Professional Values and Practice section of the Standards for the Award of QTS, and build on these. Specifically, they:

b) show a commitment to their professional development by:

- identifying areas in which they need to improve their professional knowledge, understanding and practice in order to teach more effectively in their current post, and
- with support, taking steps to address these needs.

Teaching

They continue to meet the requirements of the Teaching section of the Standards for the Award of QTS, and build on these by demonstrating increasing responsibility and professional competence in their teaching and when working with other adults, including parents. Specifically, they:

c) plan effectively to meet the needs of pupils in their classes with special educational needs, with or without statements, and in consultation with the SENCO contribute to the preparation, implementation, monitoring and review of Individual Education Plans or the equivalent.
d) liaise effectively with parents or carers on pupils' progress and achievements.
e) work effectively as part of a team and, as appropriate to the post in which they are completing induction, liaise with, deploy and guide the work of other adults who support pupils' learning.
f) secure a standard of behaviour that enables pupils to learn, and act to pre-empt and deal with inappropriate behaviour in the context of the behaviour policy of the school.

Figure 27. The induction standards.
Source: DfES, 2003.

- **How many formal assessment meetings are there?**

There are three formal assessment meetings, one at the end of each term of the induction period. Each assessment is often recorded on a national assessment proforma.

- **Who is involved in your assessment?**

Your headteacher has responsibility for making a recommendation to the LEA (or the Independent Schools Council Teacher Induction Panel for independent schools) about whether you have met the requirements for the induction period, but others are closely involved in the process, including your induction tutor, subject co-ordinators and/or key stage co-ordinators in a primary school, your head of department in a secondary school, LEA inspectors/advisers and yourself as NQT. It is in your interest to have a range of people contributing to your assessment because this means that the assessment will be a more accurate picture of your work.

- **Is the assessment done *to* you or *with* you?**

It is important that you have full involvement in the process of assessment. The national report proformas (which are reproduced in this chapter) indicate that you have a right of reply in regard to anything which is written about you. Additionally, your school is required to record the kind of support that has been made available to you. In this way, assessments about your practice are seen in the context of the support which has been made available.

- **Will I be assessed against individual standards?**

In the vast majority of cases and in regard to the consistent meeting of the QTS standards, you will be assessed against groups of standards rather than individual standards and in this way, standards can be used as broad level descriptions rather than as precise assessment criteria. It is not the intention that there will be a 'ticking off' of individual QTS standards. The induction standards are, however, fewer in number and they may be considered more as individual standards.

- **Is my Career Entry and Development Profile part of the formal assessment process?**

During your induction period, you will be using your Career Entry and Development Profile to develop a series of objectives. It needs to be recognised that this process is different from the assessment of the QTS and induction standards. The Career Entry and Development Profile can be a source of evidence that you have met certain groups of standards, but it is separate from the formal assessment process. The setting of objectives in the Career Entry and Development Profile is concerned with specific, individual paths of professional development, whereas the formal assessment of the induction period is aimed at being a broadly based judgement against nationally defined standards.

- **How much evidence is required in the formal assessment process?**

Here, the principle of clarity not quantity is important. It is in your interest to be aware of the kinds of evidence which support the formal assessments in the induction period. However, it is not normally necessary for you to collate them in an evidence file (except if you complete your induction period in more than one school), as long as you are able to provide examples of material to support judgements made on your work. This chapter will consider the types of evidence you may wish to consider in more detail.

- **How many NQTs will fail to complete the induction period satisfactorily?**

The TTA expects the vast majority of NQTs to complete satisfactorily their induction period. The prospect of failing the induction period affects only a tiny minority of NQTs. If this applies to you, it is important that you are notified at an early stage that you are at risk of not meeting the requirements, so that you have every opportunity to develop your practice.

- **What happens if your progress is not sufficient for you to be assessed as having satisfactorily completed the induction period?**

It is important to emphasise strongly that this will only apply to a tiny minority of NQTs. However, if this does apply to you, you will not be allowed to continue to teach in a maintained school (or a non-maintained special school). Additionally, you are not eligible for full registration with the General Teaching Council. You do have a right of appeal against this decision. It needs to be emphasised again that it is important to raise any concerns about the quality of support and monitoring provided by the school at an early stage (informally with the school in the first instance), so that you have the support you need to meet the induction period requirements. It is also the case that the LEA has a critical role in assuring the quality of the induction arrangements in schools in its area. Additionally, if there are very serious concerns about the education of children, headteachers are entitled to instigate capability procedures (DfES, 2003, p 117).

An overview of the formal assessment requirement in the induction period – what happens at various points in the year? **Section Two**

The purpose of this section is to provide a brief summary of the assessment process in the induction year. Along the way, some key elements are considered for you to apply to your context.

- **You will be involved in *three formal assessment meetings* during the induction period, one meeting towards the end of each term. You will normally meet with your induction tutor and/or your headteacher. The box overleaf provides an 'at a glance' summary of the formal assessment process in the induction period.**

(a) The **first meeting** will be concerned with the extent to which you are meeting the QTS standards consistently. During (or immediately after) the meeting, the

THE FORMAL ASSESSMENT REQUIREMENTS IN THE INDUCTION PERIOD

TERM 1

Ongoing professional review and observation and collection of sample illustrative evidence.

Formal Assessment Meeting 1 (end of term).
Focus: the consistent meeting of the QTS standards.
Induction tutor and/or headteacher and yourself.

If there is any indication that you are not making satisfactory progress, you are entitled to know this and to receive additional support and guidance from your school and LEA. If at the end of term 3 you have fulfilled the induction period then you are entitled to appeal against this decision

Completion of the Formal Assessment Form and headteacher submits to the appropriate body, normally the LEA, within 10 days of the meeting.

TERM 2

Ongoing professional review and observation and collection of sample, illustrative evidence.

Formal Assessment Meeting 2.
Focus: the meeting of the induction standards. Induction tutor and/or headteacher and yourself.

Complete the Formal Assessment Form and headteacher submits to the appropriate body, normally the LEA, within 10 days of the meeting.

TERM 3

Ongoing professional review and observation and collection of sample illustrative evidence.

Formal Assessment Meeting 3.

Focus: summative assessment of whether you have met all the requirements for the induction period.

Completion of the Summative Assessment Proforma and headteacher sends this to the LEA within 10 days of the meeting.

LEA decides whether you have satisfactorily completed your induction period (20 working days).

LEA notifies you, the headteacher, the DfEE and the GTC (3 working days of its decision).

report proforma will be completed, which asks for comments in relation to the standards for QTS. You are asked to provide a comment in response to the report which has been made on you and there is also a section which provides a summary of the support which you have received from your school. An example of a completed term one assessment form is provided in Figure 28. The headteacher is responsible for sending the completed report form to the LEA. Assessment proformas differ from LEA to LEA and individual LEAs are at liberty to design their own proformas using standard text provided by the DfES.

(b) The focus for the **second meeting** is the extent to which you are meeting the induction standards. A report proforma (which normally has the same format as used in term 1) will be completed as a result of the meeting. This meeting occurs towards the end of term 2.

(c) The **final meeting** takes place at the end of term 3. At this meeting, a summative judgement will be made on whether you have met the requirements for the induction period. Again, there is a report proforma to be completed as a result of this meeting. In the vast majority of cases, this is a simple statement that you have met the requirements of the induction period. In a very small minority of instances, where NQTs have failed the induction period, an alternative proforma is used which provides details of why this is the case. Examples of both these proformas are provided in Figures 29 and 30.

- **You should be clear in your own mind about the *difference between ongoing professional review meetings and the formal assessment meetings*. The former will probably be more informal and related to your Career Entry and Development Profile targets. The latter will almost certainly be more formal and, as indicated above, the results of the assessments recorded at the meeting will be reported to your Local Education Authority. It is good practice for there to be a clear, agreed agenda and for the meeting to occur in a setting where there is minimal chance of interruption.**

- **At all three meetings, you will need to give some thought to the place of *evidence*. As indicated earlier in this chapter, it will not normally be necessary for you to collect large amounts of supporting evidence but consideration should be given to using *specific* pieces of evidence to illustrate your achievement of the requirements of the induction period. These may take various forms, including records of observations made on you, your planning, assessment of children's work and your own self-assessment of your progress.**

- **It may be the case that you will complete your induction period in *more than one school* and here it is suggested that you may wish to keep an evidence file, containing sample evidence from your different schools.**

- ***If there is any doubt about whether you will meet the requirements for the induction period*, you have an entitlement to be informed at a relatively early stage in the period. It is in your interests to collect evidence which demonstrates your progress towards meeting the standards so that the assessment made at the end of the induction period is both fair and rigorous.**

department for
education and skills
creating opportunity, releasing potential, achieving excellence

Produced by Forma Consultancy on 26/9/03 – 471

NQT Induction assessment for the:

| X | End of first assessment period. |

| | End of second assessment period. |

- This form should be completed by the head teacher and sent to the Appropriate Body within ten working days of the relevant assessment meeting.
- Where tick boxes appear, please insert '**X**' into the relevant box(es).

NQT's personal details

Full name	Former name(s)
PAUL APPLEBY	-

Date of birth	DfES reference number of NQT	National insurance number of NQT
18.10.82	/	

Name of school	DfES school number
ST AIDAN'S CE PRIMARY	/

(If second period assessment):
Is this the school that reported at the end of the **first** period?　　| X | Yes　　| | No

Name of Appropriate Body receiving the report
| TRUMPTONSHIRE COUNTY COUNCIL |

| Date of appointment | 01.09.03 |

NQT's Specialism

Key stage (please specify)	KS2
Age range (please specify)	Y4
Subject (please specify)	Trained as a specialist in English and Literacy

Does the NQT work:

	part-time? (If part-time, please specify proportion of a week worked)	
X	full-time?	

Number of days of absence during assessment period	3
Number of days served during assessment period (including days of absence)	91

Recommendation:

| X | The above named teacher's progress indicates that he/she will be **able to meet the requirements** for the satisfactory completion of the induction period. |

| | The above named teacher's current progress suggests that he/she **may not be able to meet the requirements** for the satisfactory completion of the induction period. |

Figure 28. Example of a completed induction period assessment form.

Please indicate the kinds of support and monitoring arrangements that have been in place this assessment period.

X	The NQT has received a 10% reduced timetable.
X	Discussions have taken place between the NQT and the induction tutor regarding the NQT's Career Entry and Development Profile (CEDP).
X	An individualised and structured plan of support has been agreed with the NQT.
X	Discussions between the NQT and the induction tutor to review progress and set targets.
X	The NQT is familiar with both the QTS Standards and the Induction Standards.
X	Observations of the NQT's teaching and provision of feedback.
X	Observations of experienced teachers by the NQT.
X	An assessment meeting between the NQT and the induction tutor.
X	Other (please specify below)
	A planned visitation to another school regarding English and literacy co-ordination.

Under the following headings (Professional values and practice/Knowledge and understanding/Teaching), please give brief details of:

- strengths;
- areas requiring further development, even where the NQT is deemed to be making satisfactory progress (for example the Standards, or aspects of the Standards, which the NQT has yet to meet);
- evidence used to inform the judgement;
- targets for the coming term; and
- the support which is planned.

Reference should be made to the specific standards concerned.

Please continue on a separate sheet if required.

Professional values and practice

Initial discussions at the beginning of the year focused on the CEDP and indicated that Paul had a strong conviction regarding the importance of taking responsibility for his own professional development. This has been further evidenced through the term as, in particular, he has taken the initiative in arranging to observe other teachers teaching English both at St Aidan's and another local school. In the wider context Paul's professional standards are high and he is an excellent role model for pupils within his care. His teaching approach encourages an inclusive classroom.

Figure 28 (continued). Example of a completed induction period assessment form.

Knowledge and understanding

Paul has demonstrated good subject knowledge appropriate for teaching across the primary curriculum. His teaching of English, his specialist subject area, has, in particular, been informed by a convincing depth of subject knowledge that goes beyond that required for accurate lesson delivery. He has a real grasp of the subject that is manifest in his depth of conceptual knowledge. Within other core curriculum areas his subject knowledge for teaching is at least satisfactory, although my observation of a science lesson in October revealed some minor misconceptions which have since been addressed. Subject knowledge with foundation subjects not covered during initial teacher training is at least adequate and Paul works to ensure that any 'gaps' are dealt with prior to a series of lessons being delivered.

Teaching

Paul has demonstrated his ability to provide high quality and appropriately detailed planning for teaching. Whilst his planning is particularly effective within his subject specialism English, his planning within other curriculum areas is developing an increasing level of precision in regard to more focused learning outcomes. Teaching provides challenging learning experiences for all pupils and Paul is particularly adept at meeting the needs of lower ability pupils in mathematics. Across the curriculum Paul consistently demonstrates that he has the highest of expectations for pupils' learning. Assessment of pupils' learning is accurate and leads to the effective design of new learning experiences. Detailed records are kept across core subject areas, but here further clarity would be helpful in identifying key classroom assessment events. A target for next term relates to preparation for a parents' evening.

Figure 28 (continued). Example of a completed induction period assessment form.

- **At the end of each assessment proforma, there is a space for *your own comments* about the report. This is an important element of the proforma and you should be provided with time to give a considered response. You should use this box to record your views about a number of aspects of the induction period such as**

  – **whether the report is appropriate and fair**
  – **the quality of support you have received from within school.**

LEAs have an obligation to monitor these proformas and may wish to follow through any negative comments with schools.

The assessment of the standards – what to look for

The overview of the induction period section established that there are two foci for the assessment of that period, firstly the *consistent* meeting of the QTS standards and secondly the induction standards. It is appropriate that the standards are broad and, as such, open to interpretation, because in this way, it is possible to apply them to different teaching contexts and age phases. It is also the case that this broad nature can be rather bland and it is therefore sometimes difficult to see what they *actually* mean for 'me' within 'my' classroom or school. This means that, as an NQT, you may find it difficult to understand precisely what is being looked for in relation to the formal assessment associated with the standards.

One strategy to address this issue is to pose a series of key questions, which relate to areas of the standards. These questions are aimed at supporting your thinking about your professional development as you work towards your achievement of the standards. They should enable you to identify areas related to each area of the standards which you need to address, or which are a particular strength.

Provided below are lists of suggested key questions which can be used in relation to the statements of required standards for the induction period. In using them, reference will need to be made to the QTS standards. The induction standards are listed in Figure 27. It is suggested that the questions are used to help stimulate thinking about the adequacy of your performance in relation to the particular areas of standards. In this way areas of strength and weakness may be easily identified and can then be the subject of further discussion. It follows that it is not necessarily intended that the questions will all be considered at depth and individually. The questions may be particularly useful if you are less than familiar with the standards themselves.

There are two sets of questions. The first set relates to the consistent achievement of the QTS standards which is the recommended focus for the first term of the induction period. The second set is concerned with the set of induction standards, the recommended focus for the second term of the induction period.

department for
education and skills
creating opportunity, releasing potential, achieving excellence

Produced by Forms Consultancy on 15/9/03 ~ 390

NQT Induction assessment: End of the third assessment period

- This form should be completed by the head teacher and sent to the Appropriate Body within ten working days of the final assessment meeting.
- Where tick boxes appear, please insert 'X' into the relevant box(es).

NQT's personal details

Full name	Former name(s)
SUSAN OLIVER	-

Date of birth	DfES reference number of NQT	National insurance number of NQT
16.05.70	/	

Name of school	DfES school number
COLLINGWOOD HIGH SCHOOL	/

Is this the school that reported at the end of the **first** period?	X Yes	☐ No
Is this the school that reported at the end of the **second** period?	X Yes	☐ No

Name of Appropriate Body receiving the report

TRUMPTONSHIRE LEA

Date of appointment	01.09.03

NQT's Specialism

Key stage (please specify)	KS3 & KS4
Age range (please specify)	11-16
Subject (please specify)	Geography

Does the NQT work:

☐ part-time? (If part-time, please specify proportion of a week worked)

X full-time?

Number of days of absence

5	If days of absence are 30 or more, the induction period has been extended by this amount.

Number of days served during induction period, including days of absence (the induction period must be 189 school days in length).	189

Recommendation:

X The above named teacher **has met the requirements** for the satisfactory completion of the induction period.

Figure 29. NQT induction summary report form.

Comments by the head teacher:

Head teachers are invited to highlight the NQT's strengths in relation to the Induction Standards and aspects of the Standards where the NQT (although meeting all of the Induction Standards) might prioritise their professional development in their future teaching.

Susan has enjoyed a very successful induction year. Her teaching shows high levels of expectation and demonstrates the provision of high quality pupil learning experiences. In the initial stages of the year Susan encountered some challenging pupil behaviour with one of her year 10 classes. She worked hard to overcome these difficulties and achieved success. At all times her professional conduct has been outstanding.

Comments by the NQT:

It is recommended that NQT's record any comments or observations on their induction period.

I have discussed this report with the induction tutor and/or head teacher and:

☐ have no comments to make.	☒ wish to make the following comments.

I have valued the support provided for me by the staff at Collingwood High School and I have appreciated particularly the professional conversations connected with the CEDP. It was through these conversations that I dealt effectively with the year 10 class mentioned above.

School stamp/validation

Signed: **Head teacher** (if different from Induction tutor)   Date

Full name (CAPITALS)

Signed: **NQT**   Date

Full name (CAPITALS)

Signed: **Induction tutor**   Date

Full name (CAPITALS)

Figure 29 (continued). NQT induction summary report form.

department for
education and skills
creating opportunity, releasing potential, achieving excellence

Produced by Forms Consultancy on 15/9/03 ~ 361

NQT Induction assessment: Failure to complete the induction period satisfactorily

- This form should be completed by the head teacher and sent to the Appropriate Body within ten working days of the final assessment meeting.
- Where tick boxes appear, please insert 'X' into the relevant box(es).

NQT's personal details

Full name

Former name(s)

Date of birth   DfES reference number of NQT   National insurance number of NQT

Name of school

DfES school number

Is this the school that reported at the end of the **first** period?   ☐ Yes   ☐ No

Is this the school that reported at the end of the **second** period?   ☐ Yes   ☐ No

Name of Appropriate Body receiving the report

Date of appointment

NQT's Specialism

Key stage (please specify)

Age range (please specify)

Subject (please specify)

Does the NQT work:

☐ part-time? (If part-time, please specify proportion of a week worked)

☐ full-time?

Number of days of absence

☐ If days of absence are 30 or more, the induction period has been extended by this amount.

Number of days served during induction period, including days of absence
(the induction period must be 189 school days in length).

Recommendation:

☐ The above named teacher has **not met the standards** for the satisfactory completion of the induction period.

Figure 30. Form used when NQT has failed to complete the induction period satisfactorily.

Under the following headings (Professional values and practice/Knowledge and understanding/Teaching), please give brief details of:

- those requirements for the satisfactory completion of the induction period which have been met;
- areas of weakness in relation to those requirements for the satisfactory completion of the induction period, which have not been met;
- the evidence used to inform the judgement.

Please continue on a separate sheet if required.

Professional values and practice

Knowledge and understanding

Teaching

Figure 30 (continued). Form used when NQT has failed to complete
the induction period satisfactorily.

Comments by the NQT:

It is recommended that NQTs record any comments or observations on their induction.

I have discussed this report with the induction tutor and/or head teacher and:

☐ have no comments to make.   ☐ wish to make the following comments.

School stamp/validation

Signed: **Head teacher** (if different from Induction tutor)   Date

Full name (CAPITALS)

Signed: **NQT**   Date

Full name (CAPITALS)

Signed: **Induction tutor**   Date

Full name (CAPITALS)

Figure 30 (continued). Form used when NQT has failed to complete
the induction period satisfactorily.

Set 1: suggested key questions in relation to the consistent meeting of the QTS standards (for use in the recommended assessment meeting at the end of term 1)

This set of questions is related to the extent to which you are consistently meeting the standards for the award of QTS. There are three lists. Each list relates to one of the areas of the standards that should be reported on the assessment proforma. In broad terms, professional values and practice (see p. 94) are concerned with your ability to demonstrate appropriate ways of working with pupils, to communicate effectively with parents and show that you can work with a range of school staff effectively. Knowledge and Understanding (see box on p. 94) is related to the extent to which your subject knowledge for teaching is accurate. A third area, teaching, is divided into planning, expectations and targets monitoring and assessment and teaching and class management. These standards relate directly to your classroom teaching and cover areas such as differentiation, reporting to parents and assessment techniques.

Some key questions in relation to the standards for the award of QTS

Teaching

Planning Expectations and Targets

To what extent:

- are your teaching objectives matched to pupils' needs and used effectively in lesson preparation?
- do you choose appropriate resources for learning?
- do you work as part of a teaching team?
- do you facilitate out-of-school opportunities for your pupils?

Monitoring and Assessment

To what extent:

- do you use a range of assessment strategies as you evaluate pupil progress towards planned objectives?
- do you provide pupils with immediate feedback within your teaching?
- are you able to assess pupils accurately using the national assessment frameworks appropriate to your specialist age phase?
- are you able to assess and support all pupils, including more able pupils and those working below age-phase expectations?
- can you identify the levels of attainment of pupils learning English as an additional language?
- develop appropriate pupil records and report to parents and professionals on pupils' attainment?

Teaching and Class Management

To what extent:

- have you established a purposeful learning environment where there are high pupil expectations?
- can you teach your subject/phase competently and independently?
- can you teach successfully the required content of National Curriculum frameworks?
- are your lessons clearly structured?
- do your lessons use a range of teaching techniques including collaborative group work, interaction and independent learning?

- do you differentiate your teaching?
- do you meet the needs of those learning English as a second language?
- do you take account of children's interests and backgrounds?
- do you manage time and the physical classroom environment effectively?
- do you manage pupil behaviour effectively?
- do you use ICT in your teaching?
- do you set homework as appropriate?
- do you work with other staff to enhance the pupils' learning experience?

Some key questions in relation to the standards for the award of QTS

Professional Values and Practice

To what extent:

- do you demonstrate high expectations of all pupils, treating them consistently and with respect?
- do you respect pupils' backgrounds?
- do you demonstrate positive values and attitudes?
- do you communicate appropriately with parents?
- do you take part in the corporate life of the school?
- do you have an understanding of the need to take responsibility for your own professional development?

Some key questions in relation to the standards for the award of QTS

Knowledge and Understanding

To what extent:

- is your personal subject knowledge, including personal knowledge of ICT, secure for all your teaching?
- do you have an understanding of overarching National Curriculum requirements and curricula before and after your specialist phase?
  (for primary as appropriate)
- do you understand the SEN Code of Practice?
- do you know how to promote good classroom behaviour?
- do you understand (and demonstrate this understanding through your teaching) the statutory frameworks for the primary phase, including the Curriculum Guidance for the Foundation Stage, the National Curriculum and the national numeracy and literacy strategies?
- are you able to work across the range of primary subjects?
- (for key stage 3) do you understand and demonstrate this understanding through your teaching the relevant National Curriculum programmes of study, and the cross-curricular guidelines?
- (for key stage 4) do you understand (and demonstrate this understanding through your teaching) the pathways for progression at Key Stage 4 and post 16 within and beyond your subject, the national qualifications framework and the whole student curriculum?

Set 2 : suggested key questions in relation to the induction standards (for use in the assessment meeting at the end of term 2)

The second set of questions is designed to provide you with some support in making self-assessments against the induction standards (the focus for the second assessment meeting in the second term of the induction period). You will see that the induction standards are different from the QTS standards in so far as there are fewer of them

Induction standards for Professional Values and Practice	
… Seek and use opportunities to work collaboratively with colleagues to raise standards by sharing effective practice in the school	In what ways do you work as part of a team of teachers? To what extent do you make an active contribution to staff meetings? To what extent is your approach to working with others proactive or reactive? What approaches do you use to involve classroom assistants and other non-teaching staff in pupils' learning?
Induction standards for subject knowledge … Show a commitment to their professional development by: • identifying areas in which they need to improve their professional knowledge, understanding and practice in order to teach more effectively in their current post, and • with support, taking steps to address these needs	What approaches do you use as you reflect on your practice? How do you identify such areas? How do you keep up to date with developments in your subject(s) and phase? How do you develop your subject knowledge in areas where you feel less certain? How do you define 'teach more effectively'?
Induction Standards for Teaching … Plan effectively to meet the needs of pupils in their classes with special educational needs, with or without statements, and in consultation with SENCO contribute to the preparation, implementation, monitoring and review of Individual Educational Plans or the equivalent.	To what extent are you aware of the range of special educational needs within mainstream classrooms? How do you differentiate your response to this range? What particular professional skills are required for the role of SENCO?
… Liaise effectively with parents or carers on pupils' progress and achievements	What strategies do you use to liaise informally with parents? (e.g. at the beginning and end of the day) To what extent and in what ways do you take account of the audience as you prepare written reports on pupils' progress?
… work effectively as part of a team and as appropriate to the post in which they are completing induction, liaise with, deploy, and guide the work of other adults who support pupils' learning.	How would you describe your approach to managing adults who support pupils' learning in the classroom? How would others describe your approach? In what ways do you take care to induct and guide the work of teaching assistants in your classroom?
… secure a standard of behaviour that enables pupils to learn, and act to pre-empt and deal with inappropriate behaviour in the context of the behaviour policy of the school?	How would you define a standard of behaviour that enables pupils to learn? What does this 'look' like? To what extent are you able to pre-empt inappropriate behaviour? What strategies do you use in this respect?

and they demonstrate progression from the consistent achievement of the QTS standards. Progression in the induction standards requires you to be more independent in areas where you had support from experienced teachers and to take on more responsibility for some areas of teaching as opposed to merely knowing or being familiar with these. In the box you will see that the same headings are used as in set one. These headings correspond with those on the assessment proforma in Figure 28. You will also see that the figure provides the precise wording of the induction standards alongside the questions.

Section Four

Setting up the formal assessment meetings

These three meetings (at the end of terms 1, 2 and 3) are very important in the national arrangements for the induction period, because the record of this assessment is passed to your LEA and will ultimately contain recommendations about whether you have completed satisfactorily the induction period. The vast majority of NQTs will satisfactorily complete induction and here the importance of the meetings will be related to what is recorded about your teaching on the formal assessment proforma. You need to be proactive in ensuring that you are happy with the arrangements for these meetings, given that the report of the meeting will form part of your employment record.

The following points are designed to help you to be aware of important aspects related to the conduct of the meeting and cover the periods before, during and after the assessment.

Agree on the agenda with your induction tutor prior to the meeting

You need to prepare yourself for the assessment meeting and it makes sense for there to be an agreed agenda in advance. In this way both you and the induction tutor are

---

INDUCTION PERIOD – ASSESSMENT MEETING for Bethan Taylor – TERM 2
AGENDA – Thursday 18 March, 1.00 – 2.30pm

1. Review of support made available to the NQT – identify the specific elements of this support and evaluate their appropriateness in Bethan's professional development.
2. Assessment of Teaching (Planning, expectation and targets and teaching and class management) – use induction tutor lesson observation (Year 10 top set) to discuss general performance in this area.
3. Assessment of Teaching (Monitoring and Assessment) – use records of pupils' achievement in Year 8 to discuss the effectiveness of Bethan's work in terms of securing pupil achievement in mathematics.
4. Assessment of Professional Values and Practice – use Bethan's self-assessment (as recorded in her professional development file) to discuss wider aspects of professional development.
5. Assessment of subject knowledge – have areas for professional development been identified and acted upon.
6. Completion of the assessment report form.
7. Identification of areas for further consideration in professional objective-setting for term 2.

Figure 31. Sample agenda for formal assessment meeting.

clear about what is to be discussed in the meeting and what kinds of evidence are going to be cited. The agenda also establishes clearly that the assessment meeting is different from professional review meetings or feedback after observation. Figure 31 provides a sample agenda for this meeting and, as can be seen, is precise not only in terms of the headings for the different aspects of the assessment, but also in terms of the evidence which will be brought to bear on this assessment.

Who should attend the meeting?

It is normally the case that the induction tutor and yourself will attend the meeting. If there are any concerns about your progress, it would be important for the head-teacher and/or head of department to attend. However, it needs to be emphasised that, particularly in primary schools, headteachers may attend as a matter of course, regardless of whether there are any concerns.

Venue for the meeting

Where the meeting is held gives clear 'messages' about whether the assessment is being done 'to' you or 'with' you. If the meeting is held on the induction tutor's 'terri-tory' (for example, his/her classroom or office), then it is perhaps more likely that you will feel the assessment is being handed to you. It is equally important that the venue is one where disruptions will not occur and conversation cannot be overheard. Such considerations may mean a headteacher's office is the most appropriate venue, parti-cularly if you have been given release time to attend the meeting. An important part of the national induction arrangements is the principle that the assessment process is undertaken with your involvement. It follows that to hold the assessment meeting in a venue in which you feel comfortable is important.

Timings and interruptions

As part of the preparation for the meeting you are entitled to know the start and end times of the meeting and to be assured that this is protected time. There should be no interruptions during the course of your discussions, given the importance of the assessment meeting.

Evidence

It has already been established that in the vast majority of cases, it will not be neces-sary or appropriate for you to have large amounts of evidence organised in an evidence file in relation to your achievement of the requirements of the induction period. However, it is also important that the assessment meeting is informed by *specific* pieces of evidence in relation to your achievement and one approach is to use these as part of a wider discussion in relation to the induction standards. The next section in this chapter provides some further and more detailed examples of what would con-stitute appropriate evidence.

Evaluating the school's provision for you as an NQT

The purpose of the assessment meeting is not only to make a judgement on your performance against the requirements of the induction period. It is also important and appropriate that your views about the level and kind of professional support which the school has offered is discussed. Indeed the assessment report proforma requires that there is an indication of the kind of support which you have received. This is in line with the principle underpinning the induction period which states that while you will be assessed against national standards, there has to be a recognition that the induction period is an extension of initial teacher training and as such includes your entitlement to an appropriate level of support.

Clarity and honesty

At the end of the assessment meeting, it is important that both you and the induction tutor have a shared understanding of the outcome of the meeting, particularly in regard to any follow-up points for further review; for example, new objectives for the next term or changes in the kind of support which the school is offering. One strategy which can be used is to complete the assessment report form during the actual meeting, so that both you and the induction tutor are clear about what is actually being written. If there are any concerns about whether you will meet the requirements of the induction period, it is vitally important that you know about these at the term 1 and 2 assessment meetings and that you are clear about the nature of the support which will be provided to help you address these concerns. It is also important that if you have any concerns about the level of support offered by the school, you are clear about this prior to the assessment meeting. If you are not and subsequently are deemed not to have met the induction period requirements, then an appeal panel would assume you were happy with the level of support offered by your school.

Section Five

Use of evidence in the assessment meetings

The main purpose of this section is to provide you with some further guidance about the nature of evidence which may be required at the three assessment meetings. Actual examples are used which underline the points which are being made. The section is arranged in four main parts, which correspond to different kinds of evidence, namely that related to pupil achievement, approaches to self-assessment, the place of lesson observation and the possible use of the Career Entry and Development Profile.

Evidence of pupil achievement

Various sections of the QTS standards make explicit reference to pupil achievement. That related to planning, expectations and targets considers issues of pupil atainment and, more generally, states clearly the importance of planning and teaching for pupil progression. The monitoring and assessment section emphasises the need for assessment of learning to inform planning and one aspect of Professional Values and Practice is about pupils being provided with opportunities to meet their potential. These themes are carried forward in the induction standards too.

It is therefore suggested that you may wish to consider evidence related to pupil achievement at the assessment meetings, using particular examples to illustrate wider points. The following provide some illustrations of how this may occur.

EXAMPLE 1

The first example relates to Anne, who is teaching a Year 3 class. At the first assessment meeting at the end of term 1, there is a discussion relating to the requirement in the QTS standards to ensure progression in children's learning. The evidence for this is seen in children's work which is brought to the meeting.

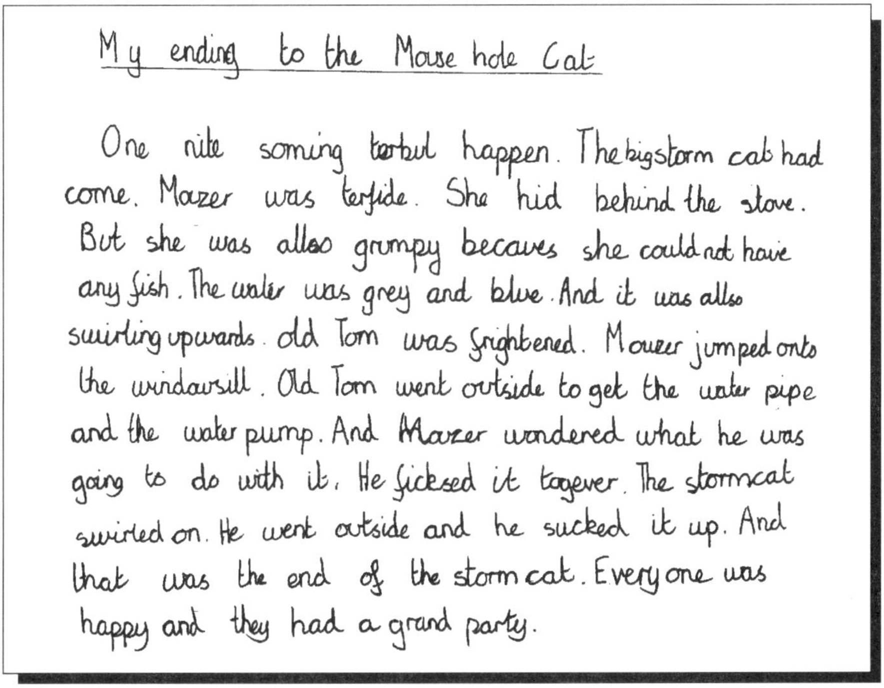
My ending to the Mouse hole Cat

One nite soming terbul happen. The bigstorm cat had come. Mazer was terfide. She hid behind the stove. But she was allso grumpy becaues she could not have any fish. The water was grey and blue. And it was allso swirling upwards. old Tom was frightened. Mouer jumped onto the windawsill. Old Tom went outside to get the water pipe and the water pump. And Mazer wondered what he was going to do with it. He fickesed it togever. The stormcat swirled on. He went outside and he sucked it up. And that was the end of the storm cat. Every one was happy and they had a grand party.

Figure 32. Dawn's ending of 'The Mousehole Cat'.

The discussion centres around two pieces of work. The first (Figure 32) was carried out at the beginning of the term and involved the children being read 'The Mousehole Cat' by Antonia Barber. From this reading, the children were asked to write, unaided, the ending to the story. The second (Figure 33) was carried out at the end of the term and involved the children being read 'The Hunter' by Paul Geraghty. Again the children were asked to prepare an ending to the story. Both activities had been set up as assessment tasks, designed to provide evidence about the children's understanding of punctuation. As can be seen from the examples, the progression is clear. In the first example, Dawn is clearly demarcating sentences using full stops and capital letters. However, in the second, there is evidence that Dawn is now able to use, with some accuracy, a wider range of punctuation including speech marks, apostrophes and commas.

There is clear evidence of progression in children's learning and this is subsequently recorded on the assessment proforma as evidence that Anne's planning has had successful outcomes in terms of progression. It is also decided at the assessment meeting

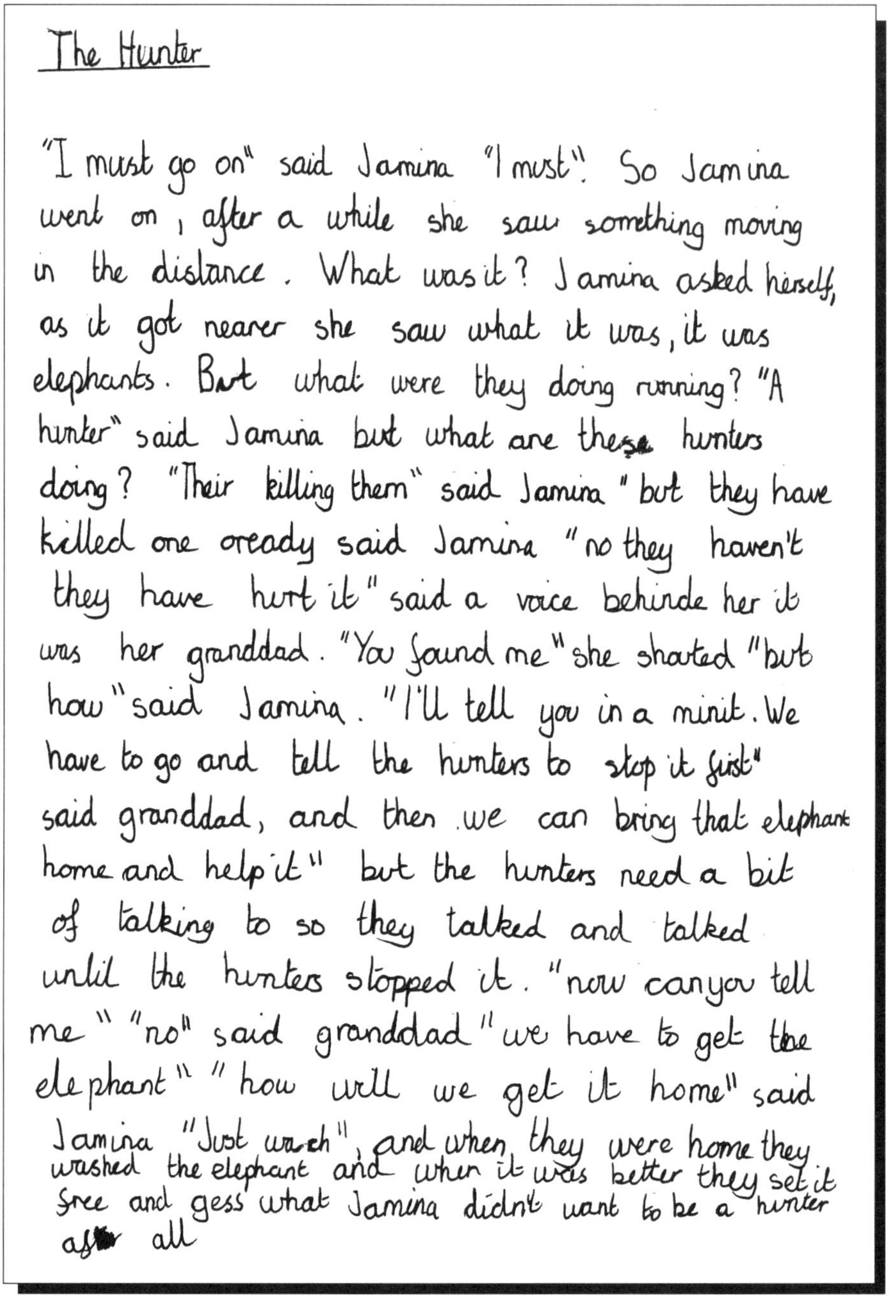

> ## The Hunter
>
> "I must go on" said Jamina "I must". So Jamina went on, after a while she saw something moving in the distance. What was it? Jamina asked herself, as it got nearer she saw what it was, it was elephants. But what were they doing running? "A hunter" said Jamina but what are these hunters doing? "Their killing them" said Jamina "but they have killed one oready said Jamina "no they haven't they have hurt it" said a voice behinde her it was her granddad. "You found me" she shouted "but how" said Jamina. "I'll tell you in a minit. We have to go and tell the hunters to stop it first" said granddad, and then we can bring that elephant home and help it" but the hunters need a bit of talking to so they talked and talked until the hunters stopped it. "now can you tell me" "no" said granddad "we have to get the elephant" "how will we get it home" said Jamina "Just watch", and when they were home they washed the elephant and when it was better they set it free and gess what Jamina didn't want to be a hunter after all

Figure 33. Dawn's ending of 'The Hunter'.

to explore further strategies and approaches which Anne may want to use in the second term of the induction year in order to take this process further.

EXAMPLE 2

The second example is taken from Paul and again concerns a Year 3 class. It is again the end of term 1, and at the assessment meeting there is some discussion about the

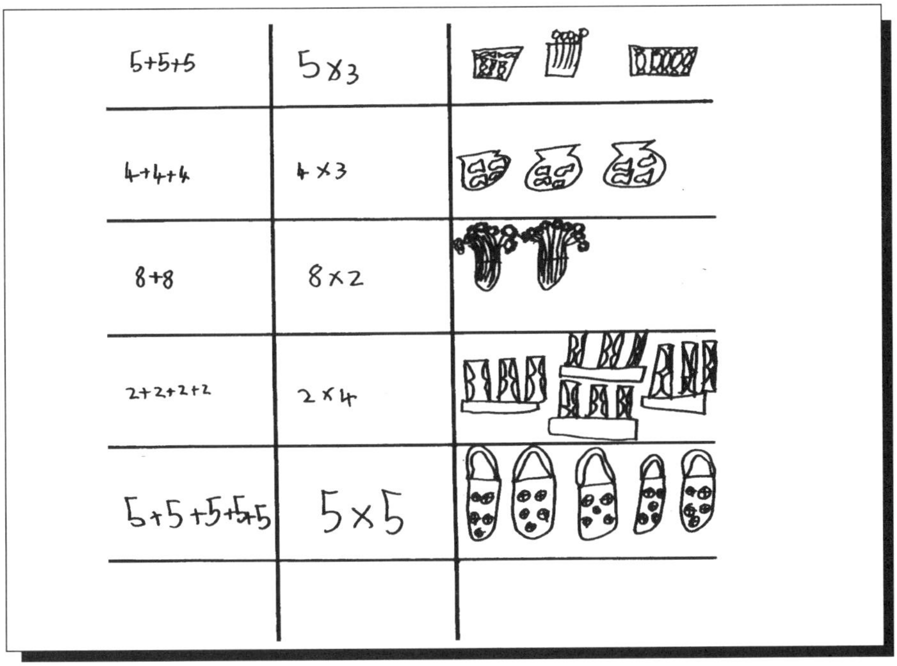

Figure 34. Philip's early work on multiplication: repeated addition.

extent to which he is setting appropriate objectives in relation to pupil achievement in numeracy. This is explicit within the QTS standards section on planning, expectations and targets. The NQT should demonstrate that they consistently set 'challenging teaching and learning objectives which are relevant to all pupils in their classes.' A particular focus for targets for the year was related to children's understanding in multiplication. At the start of the school year, a target was set for most pupils in the most able group to be able to apply multiplication skills in specific contexts by the end of the spring term.

The following evidence was brought to the meeting to show how Paul had met this particular standard. Three pieces of work show three stages of progression towards the target. In the first (Figure 34), it is clear that Philip has a concept of multiplication as repeated addition and is able to match the sum with the picture. In the second example (Figure 35), which was a result of an assessment task towards the end of the first term, there is evidence that Philip is now beginning to relate multiplication and division and that he is using pictures to provide evidence of his understanding. The final example (Figure 36) demonstrates Philip's ability to apply acquired skills in multiplication to work about multiples. This is done at a more abstract level. There is evidence that Philip has met the target which has been provided, concerning the application of skills in multiplication. The assessment meeting uses this example to demonstrate that Paul is meeting one of the key standards and this is recorded on the assessment report proforma.

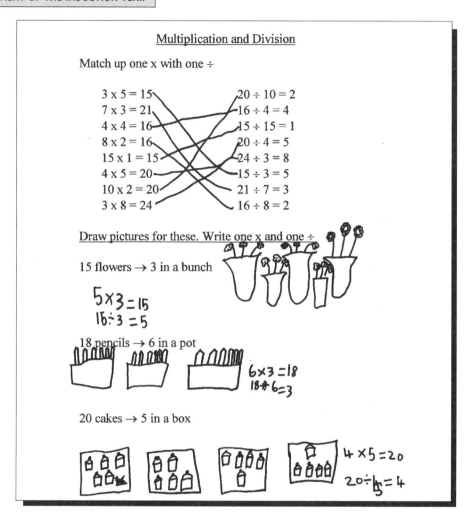

Figure 35. Philip begins to relate multiplication and division.

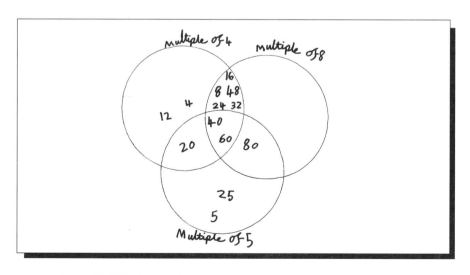

Figure 36. Philip shows he has acquired more developed skills in multiplication.

NQT self-assessment

It has already been established that you have full involvement in the formal assessment meetings such that assessments are made 'with' you, not 'to' you. Self-assessment by you in relation to your progress is a powerful way for this to be realised and enhances your awareness of the extent to which you are meeting the requirements of the induction period. Self-assessment also provides insight into whether you and your induction tutor are coming to the same kind of judgements in relation to the QTS and induction standards. It is important that you balance self-assessment with a range of other sources of evidence so that the assessment meetings consider a range of evidence.

There are a wide variety of approaches to self-assessment which can be used as evidence and there follow three examples of particular approaches which may be used.

EXAMPLE I

This example (Figures 37 and 38) makes use of the idea of significant incidents and relates particularly closely to secondary NQTs. A significant incident is any event in teaching that is thought worthy of remarking upon and then considering in a subsequent discussion with an induction tutor. It could arise from a positive occurrence in the classroom or could be seen as being drawn from a challenging or difficult situation.

In the assessment meeting at the end of term I of the induction period, Gurjit, a secondary geography NQT, wishes to demonstrate how she is consistently meeting the QTS standards in relation to effective behaviour management. This has been a focus

---

Record of significant incident
Year Group: 10
Date: 19 September   Time: 1.40pm

Details of incident
- During a whole class discussion, Robert continually shouts out, and appears to be trying to undermine my authority in front of other pupils.
- Body language indicates a lack of respect: leaning back on his chair, disturbing other pupils.
- This pattern builds up and I end up shouting loudly at Robert.
- He stops shouting out, but continues to subtly disrupt the discussion, through 'playing up with other children'.

Comments (evaluative)
- I feel that Robert's aggression was related to his feeling threatened; he may have opted out of the discussion because he didn't understand it.
- I was concerned that I was over-confrontational and this may have led to loss of face on Robert's part which led in turn to a deterioration in the relationship which I have with him.

Points to raise in discussion with the induction tutor
- Why was Robert aggressive?
- How can I develop the material which I provide so that it more nearly matches his learning ability?
- What can I do to rebuild my relationship with him?

Figure 37. Gurjit's record of significant incident: beginning of term.

Record of significant incident
Year Group 10
Date: 4 December   Time: 9.45

Details of incident
- At the end of a lesson, I conclude by asking key questions relating to glacial processes.
- Robert is clearly paying attention and his body language indicates compliance.
- I invite him to respond to a question, which he gets wrong.
- He is able to accept that he has the wrong answer.

Comment (evaluative)
- I was really pleased that Robert was able to publicly accept that he had provided a wrong answer and go on to show interest in finding out the correct response to the question without any loss of self-control or self-esteem.
- This was a new step for him in this class and represents a significant step forward.
- There was no sign of the aggression that had been such a strong part of my earlier experiences with him.

Points to raise with the induction tutor
- Why is it that Robert is now able to handle himself better in these kinds of situations?
- Is it possible to tease out actions I have taken to ensure his higher self-esteem?

Figure 38. Gurjit's record of significant incident: end of term.

throughout her first term, particularly with regard to a challenging Year 10 group. In the professional review meetings, discussions took place about various strategies and approaches to enhance the quality of classroom behaviour of this group. One strategy involved the recording of a *small* number of significant incidents which could be used in the review meetings to analyse Gurjit's progress in relation to behaviour management. It follows that it was not the intention to record a large number of incidents as this would not be helpful in relation to the in-depth analysis of individual classroom occurrences and would be unmanageable. Gurjit was asked to bring to the assessment meetings, at the end of term I, two examples of her records of significant incidents which reflected her work with the group. One of these examples was to reflect the kind of behaviour which had been typical at the beginning of the term, the other related to the situation at the end of the term. In the assessment meeting, these analyses were used by Gurjit to demonstrate the progress which had been made in the area of behaviour management.

Figures 37 and 38 show how these were recorded.

EXAMPLE 2

This example relates to Cheryl, a primary NQT, working in a large urban primary school. During the course of the second term, Cheryl and the induction tutor agreed at the professional review meeting that it would be good to have a record of 'classroom snapshots' relating to behaviour management so that some detailed reflection could occur on why there was some inconsistency in this area. A classroom snapshot is a record of events in the classroom which are perceived to be important to the NQT. They are somewhat similar to the significant incidents referred to

	CLASSROOM SNAPSHOT	CLASSROOM SNAPSHOT	CLASSROOM SNAPSHOT
MONDAY	During the numeracy lesson the noise level from John's table is unacceptable.		
TUESDAY	In Physical Education many children showed excellent co-operation skills.	Children are very slow and fussy at tidying up time. Result. Children 5 minutes late out of school.	
WEDNESDAY	The state of the cloakroom is unacceptable!	John's table remains fully on task during the numeracy lesson.	
THURSDAY	One group of children talking during the usually silent 'learning log' time. Decide to keep this group behind during playtime.	Children collaborated very well in the bridges work. Jane's group demonstrated a particularly productive approach to co-operation as they tested the relative strength of their bridges.	Assembly time. Felt unhappy that a small number of children were not paying full attention to a visiting speaker.
FRIDAY	Incident of felt tips taken from my desk during Thursday afternoon. They haven't been returned.	State of cloakroom is much improved.	

Figure 39. Cheryl's week of classroom snapshots.

Example I, but the format (in Figure 39) would be more appropriate to those primary classrooms without setting of pupils. It was not the intention for Cheryl to record all such snapshots, merely those related to behaviour management. It was also the intention for these to be recorded for *one week only* so as to give some intensity to the period of self-reflection and to make the whole process manageable. The record of the snapshots would be used to help the process of professional review for the NQT.

It subsequently became clear that Cheryl was meeting the required induction standard. However, as the use of the snapshots and their subsequent analysis was significant in enabling professional development, it was agreed that this process should be considered in the formal assessment meeting at the end of the term as evidence in relation to 'other professional requirements' and the need for Cheryl 'to take responsibility for her own professional development, setting targets for improvements'. In this sense the snapshots were used to inform objectives in the Career Entry and Development Profile. The record of classroom snapshots was used both to provide specific illustrative evidence that Cheryl had met the induction standards for professional values and practice and to plan ahead for further professional targets.

The snapshots were recorded as shown in Figure 39.

EXAMPLE 3
In this example the induction tutor and Tom, an NQT working in a secondary school, had been using a target wheel to overview the progress during the second period of the induction year. The wheel had been used once at the beginning of the second term of the induction year and again just before the second assessment meeting. The purpose of the wheel was to glean some understanding of Tom's perception of his strengths and areas for development in relation to the induction standards. It was not intended to be used as a precise measure, but rather as an instrument to raise further areas for discussion and to set more precise targets in relation to the Career Entry and Development Profile.

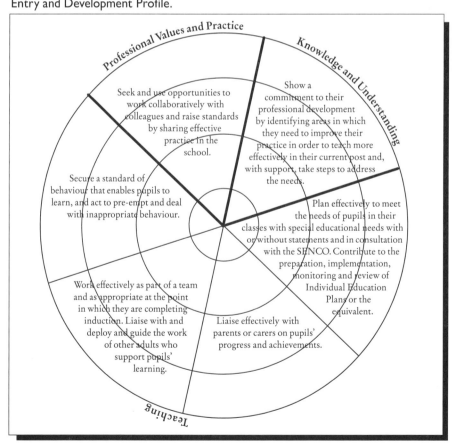

Figure 40. Target wheel for self-assessment against the induction standards.

The wheel (Figure 40) consists of the areas of induction standards statements and four concentric rings. Tom shades in the segments of the target in relation to his perception of how near he is to achieving the area of the standards under consideration. The shading should start from the outside of the circle and move towards the centre. If a segment is completely shaded then this indicates that Tom considers that the induction standard has been met. Two wheels were completed by Tom, one at the beginning of term 2 and one at the end of term 2. It was hence possible to see how Tom perceived strengths and weaknesses at the beginning and end of the second term. At the assessment meeting, the general overview provided by the target wheels was used to discuss more specific aspects of practice and, in this way, Tom felt that his views of his own performance were taken seriously at the time of the formal assessment.

Lesson observations

An important kind of evidence base for the assessment meeting is the record of observations of your teaching which will have been carried out by your induction tutor and other colleagues during the term prior to the assessment meeting. This section is less concerned with lesson observation proformas themselves than with how they can be used in the assessment meeting as supporting evidence for judgements in relation to the standards for the induction period. Chapter 3 provides some examples of different kinds of lesson observation proformas from the open to the highly structured.

It may well be the case that the assessment meeting is informed by at least two observations of your teaching carried out by your induction tutor. In many instances, however, a *moderation* observation undertaken prior to the assessment meeting may provide particularly valid evidence in relation to your assessment. A moderation observation is one where an 'outsider' to your induction year programme observes you teaching or where there is a joint observation of your work. Such observations are important in any case but particularly may be helpful to you if you have any difficulties in your relationship with your induction tutor, as they bring an objective feel to your assessment which lies outside the sometimes intense professional relationship which exists between the induction tutor and you as NQT. Moderation observations can occur in a variety of ways:

- **Arrangements could be made for a joint observation of your teaching by your induction tutor and a head of department, in a secondary school, or by the induction tutor and the headteacher in a primary school.**
- **In a cluster of small primary schools, it may be possible for there to be some cross-school observations, where the induction tutor from school A observes an NQT in school B and vice versa.**
- **In one instance an arrangement was made between an LEA and a local initial teacher training institution, whereby a tutor from the institution undertook a series of moderation visits in schools on NQTs and in return, the school-based induction tutor was involved in observing a range of final placement trainees.**

The principle is that it is to your advantage to have more than one person involved in your assessment, as this makes the assessment fair and more objective. The ideas mooted above are practical ways in which this principle can be carried forward. The example that follows provides a mini case-study of this principle.

> ### Involving a range of people in the assessment of the induction period.
>
> Sonia undertook her induction period in a large inner city infant school, where she worked in a semi open-plan reception unit. In the unit, there were three class teachers and several nursery nurses. During term 1 of the induction period, Sonia had developed a good working relationship with her induction tutor, Anne (the reception unit leader), who was able to offer her informal day-to-day support and undertook formal review meetings, using the Career Entry and Development Profile to review targets and to set new targets. Sonia developed a close professional relationship with Anne and because both Anne and Sonia knew that she would only be partly involved in the assessment process, this ensured a relaxed and productive atmosphere in the reception unit. In the school, there were two other NQTs and at the beginning of the academic year, it was decided that the assessment process for each NQT would be informed by a lesson observation undertaken by an induction tutor other than their own. At the end of November, Sonia was observed teaching by Tim, the induction tutor for another NQT and this observation was discussed at the assessment meeting, held at the end of the autumn term, where both Tim and Anne were present.

The use of the Career Entry and Development Profile in the formal assessment meetings

The main purpose of the Career Entry and Development Profile (CEDP) is to provide a mechanism for you to develop your own individual path of professional development. It follows that the CEDP should not normally be used centrally in the assessment of your induction period. The CEDP is about your own personal professional development. The assessment of the induction involves a judgement about whether you have met a range of nationally defined standards. These two things are clearly different!

Having said this, there are ways in which evidence about meeting professional objectives can be used to support judgements related to the QTS and induction standards. For example, if you set yourself an objective relating to developing the quality of your plenaries in the literacy hour (primary) and subsequently achieve this, you could cite this as evidence in relation to standards about teaching and class management.

Another way in which the CEDP can be used is to provide evidence that you have engaged in your own professional development and have taken responsibility for this. In this way, account is taken at the formal assessment meeting of the professional processes involved in the completion of the professional objectives and action plans in relation to the section of the standards concerned with 'professional values and practice'.

Section Six

What happens if I am at risk of failing the induction year?

You will know that there are two possible outcomes of the induction year. If you satisfactorily complete your induction period, you will move to full registration with the General Teaching Council for England. If you fail to satisfactorily complete the induction period and fail to meet the induction standards, you will not be eligible for registration with the General Teaching Council for England and will not be eligible for employment in a maintained school or a non-maintained special school. In this case you do have a right to appeal and extensions exceptionally can be awarded.

It has already been emphasised that the number of NQTs who fail or who are at risk of failing the induction year will be very small indeed. In the very small number of cases which fall into this category, there are a number of key actions in which you would need to be involved. Experience suggests that while the causes of professional difficulty are complex and are different in each individual case, the following actions, given commitment and determination, will help to address issues and problems. Indeed it needs to be emphasised that unsatisfactory progress in the term 1 or term 2 report does not mean unsatisfactory completion of induction. Difficulties can and have been overcome using the kinds of strategies outlined below.

Early identification of difficulties and discussion with yourself as NQT

The regulations for the induction period state that you should be observed teaching within the first few weeks of your taking up your post. One of the purposes of such an early observation is to identify any situations where there are serious difficulties, so that there is as much time as possible to address these. It is important that you are notified about serious difficulties and that there is early discussion about this. Your reaction will also be important. You may well feel angry, disappointed or let down, but it is valuable to acknowledge the reality of the situation and to be clear about what is your responsibility (e.g. to respond to advice) and what is that of others (e.g. to provide appropriate support). In these kinds of situations, it is sometimes tempting to blame others for your difficulties but this will not help to address the fundamental problem.

Evidence and analysis

A first step in addressing your difficulty is to collect a range of evidence about your practice. Such a step will enable those responsible for monitoring your progress to understand the causes of the difficulty. It may be, for example, that you are observed more frequently and with a focus which relates closely to the nature of the difficulty, such as how you are matching work to individual children, or managing children's behaviour in the classroom. Even more important will be discussions with your induction tutor. These are a crucial part of your entitlement as they have the potential to diagnose the cause of your professional difficulty, to get you to see that progress can be made and to put in place an action plan. The conversations with the induction tutor can make or break the outcome of the year and as such, the role of the induction tutor is to facilitate your development: your role is to ensure that you listen to advice and that agreed action points are carried out.

Additional support and advice

As part of your entitlement, you should have the opportunity to access sources of support and advice beyond that normally involved in the induction process. You need time to reflect and consider the nature of the professional difficulty and this should be supported by such activities as:

- visiting other schools and observing good practice there;
- attending good quality **INSET** courses related to the specific area of difficulty;
- receiving advice from outside agencies, such as advisory teachers.

Agree, monitor and evaluate targets for improvement

It is important that you have a sense of direction and purpose and targets for improvement are an important part of this process. They need to be achievable, realistic, precise and timed and you need to recognise that professional development does not happen quickly. If the right kind of targets are set and if these can be placed alongside a description of support and monitoring, then achievement will be more assured. Target-setting is the easiest thing to do badly but hard to do well, and yet only effective target-setting will help you address difficulties. It may be that, particularly at the beginning of your addressing professional concerns, short-term readily attainable targets are particularly appropriate. It will also be important that you receive regular, frequent, written and verbal feedback in relation to the targets and in terms of identifying next targets. Your role in this process will be to reflect on and evaluate your development in as constructive and honest a manner as possible. You may also wish to involve a range of people in this process at formal and informal levels.

It is hoped that the above advice is helpful in providing you with a sense of purpose, should you be experiencing difficulties in your induction year. What it cannot do is take full account of the sometimes emotionally charged atmosphere in cases of difficulty: there is a lot at stake, should you fail to meet the standards. What it can do is suggest that the path to success has an 'objective' analysis, clear supportive action, backed by precise targets and a commitment on all sides to reach for success. The case study opposite demonstrates how a problematic induction period had a successful outcome.

Claire's Case Study

Claire was appointed as the Key Stage 1 teacher in a small, rural primary school with 45 children on roll, although her training and school practice had been mainly, but not exclusively, in Key Stage 2. The head of the school taught all the Key Stage 2 children in a separate classroom and had little opportunity to observe Claire's work. She was, however, supported by a part-time classroom assistant and was able to seek advice from her predecessor, who, following retirement, continued to help at the school in a voluntary capacity. Claire's relationships with children and staff were very good but her lack of detailed knowledge and understanding of the Key Stage 1 curriculum left her at considerable risk of failing to meet the induction standards in relation to planning, teaching and class management.

In the autumn term it became clear at an early stage to both Claire and Peter, the headteacher, that there was little opportunity for an appropriate level of monitoring and support because of his full-time teaching commitment. A final placement student was allocated to the school from a local ITT provider which provided Peter with some flexibility in regard to monitoring and observing Claire and it readily became apparent that Claire was having difficulties in relation to the curriculum. Targets were set in this area and ensuing action included the development of a programme to:

- provide Claire with an opportunity to observe other schools where there was successful practice in Key Stage 1
-
- provide Claire with opportunities to network with a group of other Key Stage 1 NQTs who met for a monthly support group meeting
-
- Provide time for weekly professional discussions with the headteacher, Peter, based on observation.

Peter also contacted the local inspector/adviser (Alan) and at the first assessment meeting Peter, Claire and Alan were present. Claire was informed that while progress had been made, she was still at risk of failing to meet the requirements of the induction period. Peter voiced his concern that now the final placement student had left the school, there was less flexibility in monitoring Claire's progress. It was agreed that Alan would visit the school on a weekly basis for four weeks in the spring term, to teach collaboratively with Claire, hence giving her the opportunity to put into practice the understanding of the Key Stage 1 curriculum which Claire had developed during her observations in the autumn term. Claire found this process immensely helpful and it resulted in the development of her practice and competence in teaching Key Stage 1 children. The after-school discussion meetings between Alan, Claire and Peter helped to consolidate the progress which was now being made and at the end of the spring term Claire was no longer deemed to be failing to meet the requirements of the induction year. Early diagnosis and intensive focused intervention had helped Claire to address a serious problem. Claire continued to make progress in the summer term, supported by two further observations by Peter, and satisfactorily completed the induction period.

Chapter 5:
NQTs' Stories of their
Experiences of the Induction Year

SIGNPOST The main purpose of this chapter is to draw together the advice and suggestions in previous chapters in four stories which show how the induction period developed for four NQTs working in different contexts, in different kinds of areas and including primary and secondary schools.

I hope that the stories will give a sense of realism to your understanding of the induction period and that they may be of some use in helping you to anticipate this if you are reading this at the beginning of the year. You will see that the stories are written in different styles. Two are essentially autobiographical and the words reproduced here are the same (with minor editorial modification) as the original submission at the time of the book's preparation. These two stories are from different NQTs working in the same secondary school on the south coast of England. The third story, written in the third person, following an interview between myself and the NQT, is an account of the induction period as experienced by an NQT in a large primary school in a socially and economically deprived area of a large city in the north east of England. The final story is included by way of contrast because it refers to the story of an NQT who experienced induction six years ago. I have included this so that you can see how things have changed and developed over a fairly short period of time. It is also included to illustrate the claim I made in Chapter I, namely that the current induction arrangements have the potential to be better than ever, given the context of well-developed ITT partnerships and the concept of mentoring. Each story is presented as a whole, and then following this, there is a brief commentary about the NQTs' experiences and perceptions. As with other examples in the book, all names are pseudonyms.

Story I

Naomi Robertson (Secondary, English and Drama)

"Looking back to sitting in the lecture theatre at university, listening to the wisdom of my tutor, it is hard to believe that I have come this far.

My tutors supported me through every phase of the whirlwind, which is the PGCE, from the very first lesson, which induced tears and terror-filled nightmares, to the final assessment where I was prepared to take on any lesson, in any school! I still have the enthusiasm but, am pleased to say, a little more sense, based on experience!

Completing my CEDP was the finale to my PGCE course. At the end of my final placement I was required to present my school-based work and evidence to support the fact that I had achieved, and sustained, the necessary protocols and standards laid down by the university and for the award of QTS. This assessment was in the form of a gruelling two-hour interview. It was at this interview that I set up targets, with the help of my tutors, that would later be recorded in my CEDP. The importance of personal and professional development through target-setting was constantly addressed throughout the course.

The university prepared us for the induction year in several ways: regular interviews with tutors and in-school mentors; seminars on target-setting; target-setting feedback sessions and monitoring; lesson observations; reflective thinking and lesson evaluations. In many ways I think that this thorough preparation at university was beneficial to me in that many of the practices I learned at university have related closely to induction period requirements.

At the beginning of the academic year my mentor and I drew up a timetable of lesson observations for the term, both for me to observe and be observed. We also highlighted the order in which I would approach the targets I had set myself in the CEDP. Regular meetings were arranged and placed on a protected timetable every week. A timetable for the year's NQT meetings for all NQTs in the school was given to me. The meetings were weekly for the first two months, to be led by Sarah Bell, my induction tutor.

We were all given an NQT folder, which included information about the school and a breakdown of the targets and milestones for the induction year. I have been encouraged to keep examples of work that students in my classes have completed and relevant articles and notes from various NQT meetings. In the folder I also record each weekly meeting with my mentor, what we discuss and targets for the week. I keep a 'diary of reflection' which details highs and lows of the year so far. I have a record of each lesson I have observed and tactics that I might try. I also have a record of the lessons that I have been observed in and the feedback I received after each one.

I have a meeting each week with my departmental mentor and this is an invaluable period when I can ask questions that are department- or whole-school related. I can ask for advice and support and reassurance. During this period we will decide on targets, sometimes just for the week ahead, or for the term. For example, my target for Key Stage 4 is to standardise coursework with another member of the department. Another target is to organise and oversee a letter writing competition. Weekly, my targets are smaller, such as recently, to build the confidence of a particular student in my class who was reluctant to join in group activities. I would then feed back to my departmental mentor on my successes and record the outcome. All the targets that I set are completed with the help and support of my mentor and the department and numerous other experienced teachers around the school so that it never feels as though I am continuously highlighting my weaknesses, but actually progressing and developing.

The first assessment took the shape of a 'professional review meeting' with Sarah Bell. We discussed my practice in the classroom and we set achievable targets that I have recorded in the CEDP. My mentor also completed a written assessment of my strengths and weaknesses and I was able to respond to her comments on the reverse of the form. Although it would be easy to feel as though you are not getting anywhere, or that you have not progressed since the end of your training due to the continuous target-setting, lesson observations and assessment, I found the assessment period very reassuring. Nothing will ever compare to the first week of my first term and that feeling of complete responsibility, no friendly face at the back of the classroom where the *real* teacher sat ready to bail me out at any moment! And somehow you get used to that feeling very quickly (sink or swim method!) and although I knew that I only had to go down the corridor for help and support, it isn't the same as having someone there at the end of each lesson to dust you down and either explain where you went wrong or to praise you and make you feel like the best trainee teacher in the world. It is a very strange process because I can remember thinking, during my last teaching practice, 'Oh, I don't need to be observed again, I *can* do this!' but suddenly, when it's not there anymore I found I wanted it back. What I suppose I mean to say is that the assessment was excellent for me because it was like somebody saying 'don't worry, you are doing an excellent job, everything is going really well, YOU ARE NOT THE WORST NQT IN THE SOUTH!'

As part of my professional development I have attended several meetings arranged for the NQTs in the school such as Bilingual Learners, Hearing-Impaired Students, etc. I have also attended a weekend NQT conference that concentrated on classroom management, time management and behavioural issues. I went to a standardising meeting with my induction tutor as part of one of my targets for Key Stage 4.

I have found that there have been constant 'highs' and 'lows' throughout my year so far. There are days when I feel as though I know nothing more than I did in September and other days when I feel as though I am at one with all my classes! During the last few days of the Christmas term I felt as if I was drowning and I was tired of constantly asking questions and being unsure of myself. However, after Christmas I realised that it was just tiredness and I had renewed energy and enthusiasm. I've since learned that many teachers feel that way at the end of the first term.

My feelings on the induction year are mixed because it suits me, but I can understand why others would find it frustrating. I enjoy the regular meetings and the security of a network of support around me. I have found satisfaction in completing objectives and getting positive feedback. I enjoy having the assessment goals to work towards and am glad that my ITT provider prepared me for this year. However, I can also understand the point of view of those who say that this induction year is unfair and frustrating. If you were not the sort of person who enjoys continual analysis of your practice, objective-setting and assessments, you would find this year difficult.

I am sure that my experiences this year will help me to be a better teacher in the future. With each half-term that passes I can feel that my confidence is growing because in September I did sometimes wonder if I would make it this far. If I could have anything else, I think it would be the instant classroom presence that says to all pupils 'I'm experienced, don't mess with me!' "

Commentary

You can see that the ingredients for a successful induction period are very much present in Naomi's case. At the point of leaving ITT, Naomi felt well prepared for the induction period. She was well used to the wide range of strategies which are in use to develop practice, from observation to objective-setting. I am aware that the ways in which ITT providers prepare trainees for induction varies widely and it may be that you don't feel the sure sense of seamlessness between ITT and induction. In some cases, as for Naomi, the completion of transition point one of the CEDP was based on a great deal of preparation, including the 'gruelling two-hour interview'. In others the completion of transition point one may be rather rushed at the end of the course.

In Chapter 3, I suggest that the principle of establishing an induction programme is important if the induction period is to have cohesion and a sense of direction. It is interesting to note that Naomi had this *and* a protected timetable. All activities are included in this plan and as you can see, there is a real breadth of activity, from being observed and observing to the professional review meetings, meetings for all NQTs in the school and the NQT weekend conference.

I'm intrigued by Naomi's comment that the assessment was reassuring and I understand why she uses this word. For the vast majority of NQTs, it *will* be reassuring and positive feedback is helpful in leading to success, particularly when you feel that you are not doing very well! It's easy to get into this mentality in teaching, particularly when you are faced with the demands of the induction period which in many cases will not have the same intensity of support as many final placements.

For me the most interesting paragraph is the last but one, where Naomi writes of her overall feelings about the induction period. The reality is that your teaching will be subject to scrutiny both by yourself and others, that targets will be set and monitored, that formal assessments will be made and recorded and that you will have highs and lows as a result of this process. However, the reality also is that this process can be immensely rewarding because you will be aware of your progress in its detail and you will have the satisfaction of seeing targets met and achievements made. In order to reap the rewards, though, I believe you do need to 'go with the flow'. Individual and specific professional development cannot occur without precise scrutiny of your practice.

Alison Thwaites (Secondary, French)   Story 2

"I am a mature NQT who went back to university at the age of 37, to retrain as a teacher on a two-year conversion course teaching a shortage subject – modern foreign languages. I was a school governor for seven years (four as a parent governor and three years as an LEA governor) and chair of finance for three, so I had plenty of experience and knowledge of whole school issues before starting my PGCE. I have also been involved in the Scout Association for many years and prior to starting my course was running a Beaver Scout Colony, so I was aware of many issues involving adults working with children. I am married with three sons aged between nine and sixteen, which gives me another perspective.

I took a two-year conversion course PGCE to teach French, so when I started my course the induction year in its present shape did not exist, although rumours started flying around towards the end of my first year. At first I was really annoyed at the thought of being 'on probation' for a further year. Confirmed details took a long time to filter down to us students and the university could not answer many of our questions until almost the end of the course. I found this very frustrating and I had a very negative attitude towards the induction/probationary year.

In order to write my CEDP I had individual meetings with both of my university tutors and we came up with a shortlist of achievements and targets, from which I chose the ones I wanted to enter onto my CEDP. The university advised us to choose two subject-related and two whole school-related points, for both achievements and objectives. The subject-based ones have been useful for setting targets this year but no one else in school has ever looked at or considered the whole school ones.

I was able to visit the school before taking up my post. This was invaluable in that it helped me get to know the other people in the department and I could start looking at textbooks and schemes of work. I took part in two INSET days and spent two more days observing lessons between the end of my university course and the end of the school term. Again this was extremely useful. I spent another hour talking with the Head of Year about the tutor group that I would be given in September. She gave me a mini-sketch of each student, which was useful during the first weeks.

During the first week of term the NQTs and NQT co-ordinator, Sarah Bell, had a meeting where the NQT induction programme for the year was outlined and for the first time detailed information was given, explaining the induction standards. We also had a social opportunity to meet and talk with some of last year's NQTs, so that we could find out their reaction to the induction programme which they had followed and compare it to the one which we would be following. This was the first time that I felt that I really under-stood the induction year.

My mentor and I have one lesson a week timetabled as my mentor session and this has been the most valuable part of my induction year. Some meetings have been more formal than others, such as the formal assessment meetings, but it is always a friendly and sup-portive forum where I can discuss problems or ask for advice. For example, I knew that I needed to improve the National Curriculum level of written work by one class, so that was the focus for one session. One of the most useful mentoring sessions was the first one where my mentor and I walked around the school. He introduced me to anyone we met on our walkabout and showed me where the Year offices are, Deputy Heads' offices, Learning Resource Centre, Learning Support, etc., and he kept on asking me 'where are you in relation to the Department?' I have never got lost in the school since then. While walking, we chatted informally about the first week and my first impressions of the school and my classes. I think it helped set the tone for the positive attitude that I have towards the mentoring part of the induction year and I would strongly recommend it to any mentor.

The feedback that I receive from my mentor is one of the most useful tools for my own development. The insight and pointers from a more experienced member of staff really do help to improve your own classroom teaching. Constructive criticism helps to inform you as to what you are doing now and where you should be going. You don't know it all at the end of your PGCE and this advice and support is essential to keep you on the right track, especially in that hectic first year when everything is strange.

About half-way through the first term my mentor and I reviewed my CEDP and we set my induction year objectives. These targets were based partially on my CEDP and partially on targets that developed from lessons which my mentor observed. One target, for example, on the CEDP was to continue to develop ICT skills in and out of the classroom. On my action plan for my induction year this became the development of a self-access IT package for Year 7 pupils, which I would initially develop with my own classes before spreading it through the rest of the department. My initial review took place through a presentation about the programme, which I made to a departmental meeting, and the final review will be the assessment of how the course has worked throughout the rest of Year 7.

Another objective for the induction year set by my mentor and myself was to be fully prepared for the NEAB GCSE course. In order to achieve this I was to take part in some moderation of coursework and successfully complete the mock GCSE speaking exam. I also attended the teacher support meetings hosted by the exam board. This objective was not mentioned on my CEDP but resulted from my need to be able to conduct the speaking exams and to be more knowledgeable about the NEAB course.

I am extremely grateful for the opportunity, which the reduced timetable has given me, to observe other teachers and I would advise anyone to use this time positively. I have watched my Year 9 tutor group in drama and PE, which helped me to develop my relationship with them. I have observed other teachers dealing with pupils whom I find difficult. Sometimes I've had an insight into another way of handling these students, sometimes I've been reassured that these pupils display the same poor behaviour and attitude with more experienced teachers as they do with me. It's also been very helpful to watch other teachers within my own department.

In my opinion a lot of the induction programme after school has been repeating work already done on the PGCE course. Perhaps there is an issue here regarding the liaison process between the universities and the schools and LEAs. I feel very strongly that this part of the induction programme needs more tailoring to the individual NQTs and the gaps in their individual knowledge. My previous experience as a school governor, plus the fact that I took a two-year PGCE which gave us extra time to look into some different school issues, means that I have a great deal of knowledge that someone else may not have. Equally their experience will be different from mine and their strengths will be elsewhere. If we are serious about an individual's professional development starting with the induction year then these differences have to be taken into account at the beginning of that year. It has been very useful to have a couple of meetings where the NQTs set the agenda. I feel that the after-school sessions have worked best when they are directly related to the school in which you are working.

Taking time out to reflect is very important to me. Sometimes I do this as a quick mental review of an individual lesson and I think that we do this more than we realise but in the day-to-day survival process, it's difficult to remember your thoughts. Consequently the diary of reflection, which we've been asked to keep, has been a useful focus for this process. I really do think it's helped me work through some problems and highlight the things I am doing right and most definitely the things that have not worked. To date, this is probably the most useful tool for professional development.

I felt very low a few weeks before February half-term. Some students were displaying very poor behaviour and I didn't seem to be dealing with it too effectively. I seemed to be taken for cover quite regularly and I never seemed to have enough time to keep on top of marking. I generally felt very tired and despondent. It was at this point that we had our NQT weekend conference which certainly refocused my attention and inspired me again. It was good to share problems and successes with other NQTs away from school. It was reassuring that this seemed to be the low spot of the year for most of us and for some of the senior managers as well. I returned from this weekend refreshed, with batteries fully recharged. It was the perfect time for such a weekend.

I started off the year with a very negative attitude towards the induction year. As a mature student with family responsibilities, the 'induction/probationary' year, with its pass or fail element, was an extra burden I didn't want and didn't anticipate when I started my two-year PGCE course. Some of the activities I find repetitive, having covered them through the university programme. A questionnaire to discover the gaps in the PGCE courses may produce a more effective programme for the after-school sessions.

The trade-off between the 'induction/probationary' year and the reduced timetable works well but it is important to use this time for professional development activities, observation, reflection and not allow it to get swallowed up as extra time in which to plan lessons or mark books. This needs to be well monitored by the mentor.

One major difference between the PGCE course and the 'induction/probationary' year mentoring is that, on the former, time is split equally between subject-based and whole school issues but the induction year mentoring has been totally subject-based with the after-school sessions more focused on whole school issues. I don't think the balance is quite right. I believe that there needs to be a more formal mentor system on the pastoral side to help you develop as a tutor – maybe 1 or 2 mentoring sessions a term with your year co-ordinator. Some of the after-school sessions need to relate more directly to the impact of whole school issues on subject areas, possibly all modern language NQTs within an LEA could meet once a term to discuss whole school issues and their effect in their subject area. The lack of this support and professional development is a failing of the induction programme as I've followed it. I don't feel that the achievements and targets relating to whole school issues have been fully addressed. Will this affect my achievement of the induction standards?

I am writing this towards the end of the spring term and I would say that my views on the induction year have definitely changed. I have some reservations and can see areas where I believe adjustments need to be made but, on balance, I think that the induction year has been worthwhile. I especially believe that the extra non-teaching time has been invaluable. I hope that I've used it properly, to develop professionally, to be more reflective, more open to constructive criticism, more willing to learn from observing other teachers. I think that the induction year will set us in good stead to be able to follow the professional development path that is becoming the way forward for the teaching profession."

Commentary

Alison's story is interesting because it is rather less positive than Naomi's, although both recognise the overall worthwhile nature of the induction period. I think it is interesting that Alison uses the word 'probation' several times in her account. This raises the issue about whether the new style induction period is different or actually very similar to the probationary year, which operated until 1992. I believe that the differences are dominant over the similarities. It is true that both are formally addressed on a pass/fail basis. It is also true that the new induction period is much more precisely set up. There is an emphasis on support and monitoring and on the nature of that support and monitoring. The CEDP provides the opportunity for individually structured professional development against specific targets. As you will see, through reading Story 4, this individual element of induction was not really present in the same way as it is in the new arrangements, except in some individual cases. I believe that there is a fairly fundamental difference between induction and probation.

Another issue which Alison's story throws up for me is the issue of seamlessness between ITT and induction. The notion that some of the activities in the induction period overlap or repeat issues covered in ITT must be frustrating and I agree with Alison's suggestion of a questionnaire to define where gaps may have occurred in the PGCE course. For me, this account also underlines the issue that the most valuable part of the induction period is the part which is closely tailored to an individual NQT's strengths and areas for development. The induction period is essentially personal and individual and celebrates the fact that as teachers we all have different characteristics and qualities.

One similarity between Alison's and Naomi's accounts relates to low periods being just before holidays, one prior to Christmas, the other prior to half-term in the spring term. In my first year of teaching, I remember this very well. It's the first time you have experienced a whole year in the classroom and I can vividly remember the ups and downs of that year with variations in pupils' behaviour being a key part of how I felt about my teaching and myself. The first year of teaching is so different from even a long teaching practice and I think it is difficult to anticipate the lows of this.

The final comment I would like to make is in regard to the split in mentoring between subject-based and whole school issues. This is clearly an issue in secondary schools particularly, but it raises the question about an appropriate breadth of mentoring. It brings home the notion that the quality of mentoring is key to the success of the induction year and it raises the issue that to meet a wide range of targets, you need a wide range of mentoring knowledge, which will, almost inevitably, involve a number of different people.

Kathy Collins (Primary NQT teaching in a large urban junior school)   Story 3

I interviewed Kathy part-way through her induction year on a cold, wet winter's afternoon. I was impressed with her commitment to teaching, her ambition and the clarity of her thinking and perception. Kathy was undertaking her induction year in the same school where she had her final placement. In initial training, she studied for a BA(Hons) QTS. This was a four-year course which covered core and foundation subjects, teaching studies and a subject specialism. The fact that her induction year and final placement occurred in the same school meant that continuity between ITT and induction had the potential to be clear and unambiguous, but Kathy's developing perception of the role of objectives/targets and action-planning meant that differences were apparent.

At the end of her initial training, Kathy had two tutorials with a college tutor to identify strengths and areas for development for inclusion in her CEDP. These were based on the summative report of her final placement. Strengths related to medium-term planning, particularly in regard to incorporating English into a range of curriculum areas, the use of evaluation of teaching to inform planning, in providing children with precise and clear instructions and in the provision of a purposeful learning environment through interactive displays. Areas for development included further development of skills necessary to ensure children are made aware of lesson objectives, the development of effective, well-paced plenaries, the deployment of diagnostic assessment in reading and the continued development of behaviour management strategies. I asked Kathy about her attitude to setting objectives and establishing priorities for development and it was interesting to note that during initial teacher training, Kathy felt that sometimes objectives were set for the sake of setting objectives. She didn't see their role in developing practice. As the induction year has progressed, she feels in retrospect that her original CEDP statement at transition point one at the end of initial training is very broad and rather vague and feels this was so because she wasn't convinced that these statements would have real impact on practice. Objectives are now much more focused and Kathy sees these as being personal and achievable.

Once in school, three key areas for Kathy's objectives were established, in relation to the short, medium and long term. Transition point two of the CEDP was used to set these objectives and it was at this point that Kathy realised that the priorities for development were too open to be really effective. However, through discussions with the induction tutor, attempts were made to link the objectives with Kathy's stated priorities. In this respect a long-term objective was set in relation to behaviour management, a medium-term objective was set in regard to the pacing of lessons and a short-term objective was established which was concerned with Kathy becoming familiar with the school and its routines. The ensuing action plan can be seen (Figure 41) and it will be noticed that the objectives which have been set are precise ones bearing some relationship to transition point one of the CEDP completed before leaving ITT.

Kathy believes that the support/monitoring and assessment are all in place in her experience as an NQT, with different colleagues playing a part in assessment and support/monitoring. An example of this can be seen in relation to the long-term objective concerning behaviour management: 'to be able to implement appropriate individual behaviour strategies'. The first step was for Kathy to take the area which had been identified at transition point two of the CEDP and make it more focused, and here Kathy felt a strong sense of ownership over the process. From this objective, Kathy has been involved in a wide range of professional development activities, including observing other staff managing behaviour, background reading, attending an LEA seminar on behaviour management, using new strategies and asking for a focused observation. For Kathy, the process of observation, both of herself and by herself of others, was key. When she observed other colleagues in relation to behaviour management, she ensured that appropriate notes were taken and that a precise focus was established prior to the lesson. Kathy was very much 'in control' of the whole process of objective-setting and, because it was so personal, felt motivated by it and could see its purpose and benefit.

This theme of a personal response was carried through into Kathy's completion of the LEA Professional Development File because although this was 'imposed' from outside, Kathy was able to keep evidence in it in relation to the objectives she had set herself. For example, she has a record of sample evidence in regard to her medium-term objective

ACTION PLAN FOR THE INDUCTION PERIOD

OBJECTIVES	ACTIONS TO BE TAKEN AND BY WHOM	SUCCESS CRITERIA	RESOURCES	TARGET DATE FOR ACHIEVEMENT	REVIEW DATE
LONG To be able to implement appropriate behaviour strategies. Adopting an efficient behaviour management.	• observe other staff • background reading (Geoff Hanning) • attend LEA seminars • trial and error strategies • record progress (myself)	• children actively responding to strategies	Resources appropriate to strategies, i.e. rewards, star books	December 1999	February 1999
MEDIUM To implement effectively a plenary for every session focusing on the consolidation of each lesson.	• plan plenaries • adopt teaching strategies to use them effectively • evidence of the lesson's consolidation • plan timings of each session, i.e. intro, middle, plenary	• evidence of conclusion of lesson • lesson not 'running over time' or 'out of time' • evidence of children's feedback	• plans • appropriate resources for lesson	December 1999 (end of term)	October 1999 (half term)
SHORT To become familiar with school / class routines.	• Observe practice around school - myself and others	• know and understand the information handbook • be confident about school routines	Information handbook other staff	22 October 1999	22 October 1999

Signature on behalf of school	Date	Signature of NQT	Date

Figure 41. Kathy's action plan.

relating to pace. This includes samples of planning and observation feedback sheets. She found other aspects of the Professional Development File helpful because it helped her to see the induction year as cohesive. In this respect, there was a requirement to log INSET course attendance, including NQT training and general LEA courses, and to log staff meetings, observations and non-contact time. This latter point was particularly important so that Kathy could demonstrate how she was using the 10% reduction in teaching load to monitor her progress towards meeting her objectives.

Kathy's experience of the professional review meeting was positive. This took place towards the end of the first term and it focused largely on whether objectives had been met. Kathy brought evidence to this meeting, which was with her induction tutor and, following the meeting, she formally reviewed some objectives and established new ones. In terms of managing her own time and workload, she felt that priority should be given to objectives that could be achieved directly within the classroom itself rather than those which have an out-of-classroom emphasis.

The first assessment meeting followed an observation jointly undertaken by the induction tutor and the headteacher. She was provided with her first report and agreed to discuss any issues with the induction tutor. In Kathy's school, the first assessment meeting was very clearly focused on the observation and she wasn't asked to bring wider evidence to this meeting. The second assessment meeting in the spring term was, however, to have a wider brief. For Kathy, the most important element of the assessment meeting was its separateness from the professional review meeting which was much more tightly focused on specific objectives.

Kathy had experienced the appropriate amount of non-contact time and she valued this highly, particularly because in her school it was blocked. She felt that this enabled her to get to grips with her objectives and professional development activities in a systematic manner.

In terms of 'highs' and 'lows', the lows were at the start of the induction year. Kathy felt very stressed in the first few weeks and was aware of the Professional Development File demands from the LEA and her lack of experience in knowing how to approach routine practical matters. In this regard, a focused conversation about real, everyday situations experienced at school helped support Kathy's development in this area. This conversation was stimulated by a list of typical short occurrences (see Figure 42) and involved all NQTs in the school focusing on the specific short-term target. For Kathy, 'highs' came later on. There was a realisation that she was overworking and that she needed to pace herself better. She realised that the induction period could not be like block placement. After this, Kathy had a growing perception that she was doing well, that she was meeting objectives (which she found very satisfying) and that she was able to *use* feedback which she had been given. As her approach became more relaxed, Kathy became more effective and began to relish her teaching.

What do you do when the following happens?

You are on yard duty

- a child does a runner
- a child hurts/injures himself
- a child is in an out of bounds area
- you need a cup of tea/coffee
- a dog bites a child
- a wagon comes onto the yard
- the yard is icy
- it starts to rain

In your classroom

- a child feels ill
- you run out of pencils
- a child continuously misbehaves
- a child is continually late
- a child is continually absent (more than five days)
- a child has head lice
- a child makes a disclosure
- a child injures himself
- the telephone rings
- a child wishes to go to the toilet
- the same child wishes to go to the toilet again half an hour later
- you forget to give out school letters

- a child does excellent work
- a child tells you that he is going to the dentist during the school day
- what do you do with sick notes from children
- you lose your keys
- a child arrives after absence without a sick note
- a child refuses to do PE

In the corridor and around school

- a child (not from your class) hits another child
- a child falls over and hurts herself
- a parent approaches you and gives you earache
- the fire alarm goes off

General

- you wish to make a visit outside school
- you are ill
- you are ill before coming to school
- you have a dental appointment during school time
- your pet budgie is ill and you wish to take him to the vet during school hours
- you buy something for school use
- you are given money for trips by children, what do you do with it?

Figure 42. School routines and practices.

Commentary

One of the key issues in Kathy's story is how her awareness of the place of objectives/ targets for professional development was transformed. At college, she had a tendency to see target-setting as a paper exercise, which led to rather broad and unfocused professional development plans. Once in school Kathy was able to understand the potential of objectives to impact on actual practice and this, together with the fact that they became personal, ensured she had a very clear sense of direction to her professional development. For me there is an issue here for ITT. The skill of setting objectives for development cannot be taken for granted. It needs to be nurtured and it is important that students are aware of the rationale for setting personal targets and objectives. Why is this important for you? Why is this important now? Also the difference between targets which merely describe what will happen and those which pinpoint the professional outcome is one which is commonly misunderstood. Setting appropriate objectives is problematic but also important and, in her induction period, it is clear that Kathy now appreciates this.

It is also interesting to note that Kathy has established short-, medium- and long-term objectives. Here there is a recognition that objectives are different in nature and have different purposes. Interestingly, the short-term target was set for each of six NQTs in the school, whilst the medium- and long-term targets were specific to Kathy as NQT. This raises the issue of the difference between targets which have a personal focus and those which may relate to whole school issues or a school development plan.

A notable feature of Kathy's experience of the induction period is how her initial feelings of being stressed and overwhelmed were gradually transformed to a much more positive self-analysis. I believe that this was because Kathy was able to manage her induction period so that its elements were integral and cohesive and centred around the targets/objectives. When I met with Kathy I was very clear that she had a concept of the requirement of the induction period as a cohesive whole and these were helpful as she managed her own time and energy.

The final issue I wish to draw from Kathy's story is how there was progression in the formal assessment meetings. The first one was largely based on observation and a relatively informally structured discussion. The second one was to be more formal and involved a wider evidence base. It may well be appropriate for the assessment meetings to have a different 'feel' in each of the three terms of the induction period, particularly if the induction period is progressing well.

Story 4   Liz Ingalls (Primary)

"I wish to end with Liz's story to illustrate the difference between the induction period now and that experienced in the mid-1990s. Liz is in her sixth year of teaching and as part of the research for this book I interviewed her in regard to her experiences as a new teacher.

Liz's progress on her four-year BEd (Hons) course had not always been smooth. She had always been committed to teaching and enjoyed her actual teaching placements, where she achieved considerable success. However, for much of the course she believed that she struggled to make links between theory and practice and did not always see the point of intellectualising about teaching. By the end of the course, however, Liz was beginning to make these links between the practice of teaching and its theoretical underpinning.

At this time there was no Career Entry and Development Profile and Liz was unaware of a specific individual path of professional development. However, she was aware that Special Educational Needs was an issue for her and an area which she wished to know more about within mainstream settings. Because target-setting was not part of professional culture at this time, Liz did not really 'open the door' to identify specific areas for her professional development within the broad area of SEN. In much the same way, Liz was aware of professional issues in her induction year but sometimes found that she didn't have the opportunity to articulate them in a systematic manner. She knew that her teaching was good but was unaware of *why* it was good. Opportunity for her to develop her own understanding was based on 'ad hoc' professional conversations with teachers and tutors, rather than related to specific goals. While this had the advantage of not atomising teaching and learning into a large number of components, it had the disadvantage that professional development was unstructured and 'by chance'.

At the end of her course Liz returned to her home area and began to apply for jobs. She had a number of unsuccessful interviews but eventually was successful at her current school. Liz describes the formal interview itself as being difficult but she felt comfortable with her work in the classroom prior to the interview and this and the informal group interview created a strong positive impression. She succeeded in securing her first post which she began during the first week after half-term in the autumn term. She taught a Year 4 class, which she found challenging at first in a team-teaching situation with an experienced teacher. Liz was able to use her drama specialism in other classes in the school.

There were two elements to Liz's induction programme, internal and external. The external induction programme was run by the LEA. This had two main aspects, the first being courses for NQTs on planning, Special Educational Needs and behaviour management, which Liz describes as being rather general and repetitive of some aspects of her ITT course. The second aspect, however, was really useful and involved an LEA adviser seconded from a local school to support NQTs coming into Liz's classroom for half a day a week. The usual pattern was for the adviser to take the bulk of the class while Liz worked with small groups of children. There were plenty of opportunities here for modelling and collaborative teaching and the details of the role were planned from week to week. As time went by, targets were met (although not in the form of an action plan) and it was at this point that Liz was able to pick up on her understanding of SEN issues and develop her practice in this area.

Internally there were two NQTs in Year 4, Liz and her colleague Tim. There was much informal unstructured support and in this way they were given release time to support each other. The two NQTs had an assigned mentor who met with them on a regular basis but the support was mostly informal and 'reactive' to events, rather than proactive in terms of fulfilling a set agenda. There were also formal observations of teaching at various points in the year from the mentor, the headteacher and a second LEA adviser. These observations were helpful in providing positive, constructive feedback, but they did not relate closely to other aspects of the support. At the end of the year, there was an informal interview with the headteacher, which was the entitlement of all teaching staff in the school, including the NQTs.

Liz's overriding impression of her induction year is of being in a very supportive environment where there was a great deal of informal monitoring. Professional development was somewhat ad hoc, although the visits from the teacher seconded to the LEA were very helpful and specific. There was no formal assessment of the year and Liz is far from convinced that it is necessary. For her, the whole period was fairly relaxed and informal, but at the same time she feels that she learnt a great deal from her experiences."

Commentary

As I was interviewing Liz, I reflected on some of the main similarities and differences between the induction period then and now. I suspect that while there will still be variations, the CEDP and the new arrangements may mean that there is more uniformity in the experience of an NQT in 2000 and beyond. It strikes me that the external support for Liz was particularly well developed and far more than most NQTs will experience in the current induction arrangements. In contrast, her internal support through a mentor was not as well developed as it would be today. Even six years ago mentoring was not ubiquitous in primary schools.

It is true that Liz's experience was probably more informal and low key than that experienced by many NQTs. There were no induction standards, Career Entry and Development Profiles, action plans and objectives and no formal assessment either. It is equally true that the expectations of what should be achieved in the induction period are much higher than six years ago. Professional development should not be ad hoc but systematic and planned over a period of time. The 10% reduction in teaching load has to be a good thing, because it recognises that you need time and space for professional development activities in your induction period. The question is whether the tighter regulatory framework and enhanced expectations are prices worth paying for a better quality of entitlement in the induction period. In my judgement they certainly are. The reality is that the teaching profession is increasingly performance driven and standards orientated. To be aware of one's performance in the induction period and to be able to plan for the development of classroom skills are initially important and, many would argue, professionally rewarding.

In June 2000 I had the privilege of organising a conference week for final year primary undergraduate trainees who were about to leave St Martin's College, Ambleside campus, to enter the teaching profession. During the week we considered a wide range of issues and experienced a number of college and outside speakers. The week started with an input on the nature, purpose and structure of the induction period and an NQT from a previous student year group made an important contribution here. Students received input on the role of governors, the DfEE circulars related to child protection, conditions of service and professional conduct, and engaged in seminars about these topics. The week ended with a memorable visionary talk from Patrick Whittaker, Education Consultant. Focusing on 'stories' and 'questions', Patrick provided the conference with a vision of the essence of teaching and reminded us why we do what we do.

It is true that as an NQT and a teacher you may well visit 'induction land', 'performance management land', 'SATs land', 'fast track land', 'targets land', 'benchmark land', 'baseline assessment land', 'Curriculum 2000 land' and even the 'land of PANDAS'. All these are relevant places to go to, but in visiting them please do not forget the values, beliefs and motivations which were important to you when you made the decision to teach. *Succeeding in the Induction Year* is not about complying with national regulations but about mediating and interpreting these so that your experience of the induction year complements rather than contradicts your persona as a teacher. Good luck!

Bines, H. and Boydell, D. (1995) Managing support for newly qualified teachers in primary schools, *Mentoring and Tutoring*, **3**(1) pp. 57–61.

Bleach, K. (1998) Off to a flying start? Induction procedures for newly qualified teachers in secondary schools in the Republic of Ireland, *Mentoring and Tutoring*, **6.1**(2) pp. 55–61.

Bolam, R. (1994) Recruitment and induction of beginning teachers, in T. Husen and N. Postlethwaite (eds) *International Encyclopaedia of Education*, 2nd edition, Oxford, Pergamon Press.

Bolam, R., Baker, K. and McMahon, A. (1975) *The Teacher Induction Pilot Schemes (TIPS) Project: a National Evaluation Report*, Bristol, University School of Education.

Bolam, R., Clark, J., Jones, K., Harper-Jones, G., Timbrell, T., Jones, R. and Thorpe, R. (1995) The induction of newly qualified teachers: where next? *British Journal of In-service Education*, **21**(3) pp. 247–259.

Calderhead, J. (1991) The nature and growth of knowledge in student teaching, *Teaching and Teacher Education*, **7**(5/6) pp. 531–535.

Calderhead, J. and Lambert, J. (1992) The induction of newly appointed teachers. Papers prepared for the General Teaching Council, England and Wales, Slough, NFER.

Calderhead, J. and Robson, M. (1991) Images of teaching: student teachers' early conceptions of classroom practice, *Teaching and Teacher Education*, **7**(1), pp. 1–8.

Calderhead, J. and Shorrock, S. B. (1997) *Understanding Teacher Education*, London, Falmer.

Capel, S. (1998) The transition from student teacher to newly qualified teacher: some findings, *Journal of In-service Education*, **24**(3) pp. 393–409.

Carré, C. (1993) The first year of teaching, in N. Bennett and C. Carré (eds), *Learning to Teach*, London, Routledge.

Collins, M. (1969) *Students into Teachers*, London, Routledge and Kegan Paul.

DES (1972) *Teacher Education and Training*, London, HMSO (The James Report).

DES (1982) *The New Teacher in School*, London, HMSO.

DES (1987) *The New Teacher in School*, London, HMSO.

DES (1992) *Induction of Newly Qualified Teachers*, Administrative Memorandum 2/92, London, HMSO.

DFE (1992) *Initial Teacher Training: Secondary Phase*, Circular 9/92, London, DFE.

DFE (1993) *The Initial Training of Primary Teachers*, Circular 14/93, London, DFE.

DfEE (1998) *Teaching: High Status, High Standards, Requirements for Courses of Initial Teacher Training*, Circular 4/98, London, DfEE.

DfEE (1999) *The Induction Period for Newly Qualified Teachers*, Circular 5/99, London, DfEE.

DfEE (2000) *The Induction Period for Newly Qualified Teachers*, Circular 0090/2000, London, DfEE.

DfES (2001) *The Induction Period for Newly Qualified Teachers*, Guidance 582/2001, London, DfES.

DfES (2003) *The Induction Support Programme for Newly Qualified Teachers, Guidance 0458/2003*, London, DfES.

DfES/TTA (2002) *Qualifying to Teach: Professional Standards for Qualified Teacher Status and Requirements for Initial Teacher Training*, London, DfES/TTA.

Doyle, W. (1986) Classroom organisation and management, in M. C. Wittrock (ed.) *Handbook of Research on Teaching*, New York, Macmillan.

Evans, N. (1978) *Beginning Teaching in Professional Partnership*, London, Cassell.

Hagger, H., Burn, K. and McIntyre, D. (1993) *The School Mentor Handbook*, London, Kogan Page.

Lee, M. (1993) Editorial, *British Journal of In-Service Education*, **19**(1) pp. 3–4.

McNair Report (1944) *Teachers and Youth Leaders*, London, HMSO.

Moyles, J., Suschitzy, W. and Chapman, L. (1999) *Teaching Fledglings to Fly …?*, London, ATL.

OFSTED (1993) *The New Teacher in School*, London, HMSO.

Simco, N. (1995) Professional profiling and development in the induction year, *British Journal of In-service Education*, **21**(3) pp. 261–72.

Simco, N. (1997) An investigation into the classroom activity generated by pre-service teachers. Unpublished PhD thesis, Lancaster University.

Simco, N. and Sixsmith, S. C. (1994) Developing a mentoring scheme in primary initial teacher education, *Mentoring and Tutoring*, **2**(1) pp. 27–31.

Simco, N. and Sixsmith, S. (1999) The Teacher Training Agency's Career Entry Profile: is ITT and induction now seamless? Paper presented at the British Educational Research Association Annual Conference, University of Sussex.

Sutherland, S. (1997) *Teacher Education and Training: A Study*, London, National Committee of Inquiry into Higher Education.

Taylor, J. K. and Dale, I. R. (1971) *A Survey of Teachers in Their First Year of Service*, Bristol, University of Bristol, School of Education Research Unit.

Teacher Training Agency (1999a) *Supporting Induction of Newly Qualified Teachers*, London, TTA.

Teacher Training Agency (1999b) *Induction Credit Feasibility Study, Summary of Key Findings*, London, TTA.

Teacher Training Agency (2000) *Career Entry Profile, Notes of Guidance and Standards*, London, TTA.

Teacher Training Agency (2003a) *Career Entry and Development Profile*, London, TTA.

Teacher Training Agency (2003b), *Supplementary Support Materials, Career Entry and Development Profile*, London, TTA.

Tickle, L. (1994) *The Induction of New Teachers: Reflective Professional Practice*, London, Cassell.

Thompson, M. (1991) Induction: a view from the teachers' organisation, *British Journal of In-Service Education*, **17**(1) pp. 229–36.

Totterdell, M. Heilbronn, R., Bubb, S. and Jones, C. (2002) *Evaluation of the Effectiveness of the Statutory Arrangements for the Induction of Newly Qualified Teachers, Research Report* (RR338), Nottingham, DfES.

Turner, M. A. (1982) The deep end, *Times Educational Supplement*, 29 November.

Turner, M. A. (1994) The management of the induction of newly qualified teachers in primary schools, *Journal of Education for Teaching*, 20(3) pp. 325–41.

Wragg, E. C. (1993) *Primary Teaching Skills*, London, Routledge.

Wragg, E. C. and Brown, G. (1993) *Explaining*, London, Routledge.